AMONG THE LOST

AMONG THE LOST

Book Two of In Dante's Wake

Seth Steinzor

Fomite
Burlington, VT

Poems copyright 2016 © by Seth Steinzor

All rights reserved. No part of this book may be reproduced in any form or by any means without the prior written consent of the publisher, except in the case of brief quotations used in reviews and certain other noncommercial uses permitted by copyright law.

ISBN-13: 978-1-942515-05-0
Library of Congress Control Number: 2016953061

Fomite
58 Peru Street
Burlington, VT 05401
www.fomitepress.com

Cover Art - Jennifer Gammon
To see more of Jennifer's art,
visit https://squareup.com/store/jennifergammonart/

Acknowledgements and Dedication

Marc Estrin, thank you for your unfailing interest in this project and for your faith in it, which at times has exceeded mine. Rennie McQuilkin, thank you for your skillful literary midwifery, and for the grace with which you let go. Thank you to Joan Price fot the title to this book' to Hele Pashgian, John Hough, Libby Chaney, and Kate Christensen, for helping me recover the historical Vicky Carter; to Susan Weiss, for your sagacity, whimsy, and friendship; to Andrea Pappas, for showing me the beautiful cathedral of your faith; to Michael Breiner for the monthly Flynndog readings, and to the community of poets you bring together there, a constant source of comradeship and inspiration; to Lisa Lax, for more than I can say; and, last but most, to Mira and Isaac, for everything -— this book is dedicated to you, kids.

The body! It is the lawyer's term for the restless, whirling mass of cares and anxieties, affections, hopes, and griefs that make up the living man.

    Charles Dickens
    "The Posthumous Papers of the Pickwick Club," ch. XLV

'Identity?' said Jack, comfortably pouring out more coffee. 'Is not identity something you are born with?'
'The identity I am thinking of is something that hovers between a man and the rest of the world: a mid-point between his view of himself and theirs of him – for each, of course, affects the other continually. A reciprocal fluxion, sir. There is nothing absolute about this identity of mine. Were you, personally, to spend some days in Spain at present you would find yours change, you know, because of the general opinion there that you are a false harsh brutal murdering villain, an odious man.'

    Patrick O'Brian
    "Master and Commander" Chapter Eight

A kluger farshtait fun ain vort tsvai. ("A wise man hears one word and understands two.")
    Yiddish proverb

and here I sit so patiently
waiting to find out what price
you have to pay to get out of
going through all these things twice

    Bob Dylan
    "Stuck Inside of Mobile with the Memphis Blues Again"

Contents

Foreword	
Bardo	1
Canto I: Arrival	3
Canto II: Dressing for the Occasion	11
Canto III – The Excommunicated	18
Canto IV – The Tardy to Waken	23
Canto V – The Lately Repentant	29
Canto VI: In the Clouds	36
Canto VII: Close Encounters	43
Canto VIII: Delinquent Leaders	49
Canto IX: Follow the Lede	57
Canto X: Statuary But Not Unmoving	63
Canto XI: We're Talking Proud!	70
Canto XII: Out of Your League	77
Canto XIII: Envy	83
Canto XIV: Fathers	91
Canto XV: What Cannot Be Shared	97
Canto XVI: The Wrathful	102
Canto XVII: Smoke and Morals	112
Canto XVIII: Loose Ends	118
Canto XIX: The Avaricious, Part One	126
Canto XX: The Avaricious Get Another Part	132
Canto XXI: Statius	139
Canto XXII: Cheerios	146
Canto XXIII: Swallow	153
Canto XXIV: We Leave the House of Gluttony	159
Canto XXV: Red Jacket	164

Canto XXVI: Lust	171
Canto XXVII: The House of Loss	177
Canto XXVIII: The Earthly Paradise	183
Canto XXIX: Off the Wheel	190
Canto XXX: The Bug-eyed Gardener	198
Canto XXXI: The Song of Grief	204
Canto XXXII: Her Long and Slender Touch	209
Canto XXXIII: On the Beach	217

Foreword

I began this work, a trilogy of which the book you hold in your hands is the second part, with the aim of inhabiting the world that Dante presented to us in his Commedia. The idea was to demonstrate what fascinates me in it. I have loved Dante's work for forty years, an affection many friends have found inscrutable. Although I am neither a critic, historian, theologian, philosopher, nor scholar, I am a poet; since Dante chose poetry as the medium through which to speak to me, it seemed apt to use that modality to express what I see when I look through his window. There, he says, look, a tree. I look where he is pointing and try to describe it in terms that make sense to me. Sometimes it looks like a tree. Sometimes it looks like a bowl of poinsettias. Sometimes I can't see anything growing at all on that bald mountaintop, and then I try to find out why he would say he sees a tree there.

This process, difficult though it was, served me well in *To Join the Lost*, the first book of the trilogy, based on L'Inferno and like it devoted to a journey through evil. Although it wasn't quite as simple as substituting modern villains for medieval ones, our modern self mutilations look reasonably similar to those of seven hundred years ago, for the most part. Technical innovations to the side, and allowing for shifts in emphasis as to the objects of our opprobrium, we have not added much to the basic repertoire of kill, maim, betray and steal. Easy familiarity is probably at least in part why L'Inferno is the most enduringly popular of Dante's books. Where he saw a hemlock, often I saw hemlock, too. Or perhaps an oak, or a palm – in any event, usually something of an arboreal character. Our different notions as to how it came to be there, and why we might differ as to the species of what we observed, formed a basis for our implicit dialogue. On the several occasions when his finger, quivering with passion, indicated nothing that had any obvious place in my experience, it was exciting to engage in the more intimate conversation that always led me to an image of what he was talking about. At such moments I felt closest to our common humanity and to his living presence.

Among the Lost, almost in its entirety, springs from that latter sort of experience. It is based on Dante's Purgatorio. In Dante's day, Purgatory was the mountain where souls not damned went after death to cleanse themselves of sin in preparation for entering Paradise. I am sure that there are people walking on the earth today, perhaps many, who resonate to the theories of pedagogy and human development underpinning Dante's vision of this redemptive process. I am not one of them. Blame Freud and Marx and their progeny, if you will. Whereas the basic topography of Hell has remained largely stable since Dante's time, in Purgatory there have been far more devastating earthquakes than that caused to Dante's underworld when Jesus' resurrection shook the place.

I remember a job I had in the 'sixties in the warehouse of a knitting factory. On breaks and at lunch time I would sit in a corner, reading Das Grundrisse. It was mostly incomprehensible to me, but I puzzled doggedly through it, seeking clues to my situation. They always seemed just beyond the next paragraph. I remember a psychology course I took my freshman year in college, seeking explanations of the unaccountable weirdness of human behavior beyond what dialectical materialism could offer. It was all about sodium ions. I found this, too, unsatisfying. The point, however, is not that there were no answers, but that there is no way to reconcile the terms of these enquiries with Dante's vision of salvation through a one-size-fits-all, ascending cycle of punishments and expiations. It had not been so hard to locate the features of my mental universe that correspond or answer somehow to the spiritual impulses driving his, but here we were at a stand. To join him on the ground of his understanding of human mental and moral development would have required me to abandon most of my intellectual apparatus. I was forced to accept that part of knowing him involved knowing that in some ways we are alien to one another. Not only could I not see the tree, I could not see the possibility of anything like it, not in reality.

But here's the rub: Dante's writing is about nothing if it is not about reality, in every detail, on every level. When he describes a person, that person breathes on the page. When he tells you that the angry work out their anger from within a roiling black cloud of smoke, or that the envious transcend their envy through having their eyelids shown shut with wire, or that we leave lust behind only by having it burnt out of us, he is speaking undeniable simple and direct truth. His words spring from the profoundest sort of engagement with being in all its aspects - physical, emotional, psychological, social, political – of which a human mind is capable; and it was a mind of surpassing sensitivity, power and clarity. He must be taken seriously, even when the things he says have become impossible to take seriously as living ideas.

In my intercourse with Dante, our implicit dialogue already was motivated by disjunctions and cognitive dissonance, and this had led, as I have said, to some of its most intimate moments. Now that intimacy broadened, with paradoxical effects, as the reader will see. In any healthy, loving relationship, greater intimacy is accompanied by greater freedom; a statement with which I am sure that Dante would agree. It is a large part of what his work is all about. As in To Join the Lost, Dante is present behind every line of Among the Lost, but in this latter book he is farther to seek.

Although you do not need to have read To Join the Lost in order to enjoy this book, there are some things that it will be helpful for you to know. In To Join the Lost, seven hundred years have elapsed since Dante's first journey through Hell at the heels of the Roman poet Virgil. Dante now is acting as guide for someone with my name and much of my history, enlisted for this task by Victoria, a girl I knew many years ago in my teens, who died in a car crash. (For those inclined to confuse art with autobiography, I will mention as a token of warning that the girl I knew in "real life," whom I loved and who in fact did die in a car crash, would have been appalled to be called Victoria. She hated the name.) Dante's mission is to bring me to her, and the route leads through Hell.

As with any great city, the passage of time has wrought some changes. Dante's original tour culminated in exiting the underworld by climbing out, hand over hand, up Satan's hairy body, which had penetrated through the earth to the icy infernal regions at its center like a stick in a candy apple. Yes: Hell had frozen over as early as the thirteenth century. The myth of Lucifer remains alive enough in us that it continues to evoke a constellation of powerful responses, and indeed Dante's use of it in his book was particularly wise and compelling; but fidelity to what I like to think of as a higher honesty forbade me to employ the same escape route. (We can believe in the same effects without concurring in the same prime movers.) Suffice it to say that whereas Virgil carried Dante up on his back like a rock climber hauling a rucksack, Dante and Seth jump into a well, holding hands. They arrive, as did Dante and Virgil, on the outskirts of Purgatory, where this book picks up the story.

Bardo

Three quarters of an hour with nothing to do
but fall. The fabled fall from grace
has shafted our world's heart; and where it drilled
we fell, eighteen thousand miles
an hour through the place beneath all places;
one weightless instant; slowing then
concurrently with increasing ponderosity;
hovering – just at that moment when my
hundred ninety pounds eleven ounces was
poised and ready to drop back down the

bottomless pit, Dante said, "Here it is!"and
flung an arm around me like a
lifeguard saving a drowning swimmer and yanked me
sideways where instead of bashing the
tunnel's rocky wall I landed ungently
face down, kneecaps sorely scraped on
hard-packed dirt in utter blindness. I wondered,
when I'd recovered enough to wonder,
why he'd plunged me into this cave, not knowing
we had turned towards the light.

Canto I: Arrival

We navigated sightlessly, by feel,
and not only fingers but shoulders, elbows,
and jarringly twice my forehead supplemented
Dante's "This way!" and "Over here!"
and "Mind that drop-off to the left!" in stumbling
forward through the rocky tunnel,
until, negotiating a series of switchbacks,
we began to meet unbaffled
photons bouncing towards us. The merest hint of
visual tone gave form to the blackness,

insinuated, "Here's the next turn."
So it was, and the next announced
itself a bit more clearly, and the grey of the
next held discernible textures and tinges
my starving eyes rioted among.
Soon, ahead, a yellow oval
poured its honey on us, and the memory of the
bitter, murky shades below
thinned and paled; so rich, that light, my body, my
sense of my body, thinned and paled; my

feet no longer felt the dirt beneath them.
This memory bobbed to the surface: a

summer night, the cottage's porch lights' amber
streaks each side of the full moon's silver
bar that crossed the pond to pierce me where I
floated, on my back, night-dazzled.
These lights, blurred through half-closed eyelids, shift and
now I blink and here I am. A
floor lamp turned low glows in the corner.
At the other, darker end of the

couch, a table with lamp and magazines that
no one's reading. Dominating this
small, square room, a hospital bed. Upon it,
her body dominated by
her belly, lies a woman giving birth.
A nurse is checking her dilation,
and, although her husband's fingers also have
entered her there, his tender inquiring
exploration did not probe so deep or
so insistently. She groans.

The husband, suddenly weak-kneed, totters from his
station by her shoulder, where he'd been
offering ice chips, caresses, and encouragement.
Slowly, he descends to the couch as if
someone had let the air out, closing his eyes when
his wife groans again. He does not
see the nurse withdraw her latex-covered
digits, glance at him amused, and

whisper to the laborer, "Not yet. But soon."
Which he does not hear. The nurse,

leaving the room, reflects on the weakness of men and
how her feet ache despite her new sneakers.
The room is quiet. The mother floats adrift
on waves that always recede just at
the moment they are about to overwhelm her,
and each one is bigger than the last.
Over her terror and fatigue she rides,
exhilarated, her mastery constantly
threatened. What came so slowly bursts upon her.
During the months of advent, she had

endured her body becoming a stranger's body:
heavier, hungrier, breasts enlarging
as they hadn't since she was sixteen,
aching back, the urge to pee;
lying in bed at night unable to sleep and
gazing down her rolling torso
at this eminence, this nunatak.
Now she must expel a self as
intimately alien as her dreams, a
process she'll describe much later,

when she's asked, as "shitting a watermelon."
Feeling he should do something
when the nurse is gone, the husband resumes his

station by her shoulder. Massage? She
does not want to be kneaded. Whispered endearments
piss her off. An invitation to
breathe in rhythm elicits a sharp, "You're hovering!"
Fearful of her anger, he stands off
from her bed a bit and, stolid as a
coastal rock, he breaks the waves she

flings at him. So the nurse, returning,
finds them. This time, the father stays put
(but looks away) and fortitudinously
bears the fingering and the groaning;
congratulates himself upon it, knowing
no one else will. The nurse says, "Now."
He moves to his wife and takes her hand in his.
She clutches tight. "Relax," he says,
"and put the effort where it counts." She nods,
slowly, once, twice. Her fingers

limpen. Then the tide returns, the surf is
up, it's Malibu and Fundy
all at once. She rides enraged, exultant.
"Push! Push!" the others urge.
It maddens her more: after all these helpless months, these
hours of being told not yet we'll
tell you when, as if she needed to be
urged at last to act, to be.
Eyes wide, she glimpses Dante near the ceiling,

thinks that he's her long-dead dad.

Bearing down. And then it ebbs. The husband
lays a damp cloth on her forehead.
Quiet, empty minutes. Energy running
through her body begins to fill them.
This time, she is readier, greets it calmly.
It thrills throughout her thighs and groin
and belly, gathering force beyond the fiercest
orgasm. "Huff! Huff! Huff!"
she and the husband gasp in unison, and
he begins to cry at the little

he can do, while she, with an athlete's timing,
catches the swell at its awful crest, her
every muscle wrapped around and squeezing
back against this being swelled
within her, howling now at the very end and
sobbing because again it leaves her
unfinished. The husband thinks her cries mean pain,
and hurries to dampen another towel.
When he returns, the next one's just beginning.
So it goes, eleven times more. The

nurse is counting. The mother's lost in rhythm and
sweat, her long blonde ringlets lank. The
husband metronomically swings between her and the
sink, redampening washcloths. Her strength's on the

ebb, she feels it, but at the same rate now she
finds her groove: her body calls and
she responds like a gospel choir to the solo,
oh! such power! hallelu!
So her will is joined to the greater will that is
also hers, eleven times, and

on the twelfth the crazing pressure rends her
barely wide enough, it burns! She's
torn! She'd rip herself in half to tender this
life! And in the widened hole
between her legs, a hairy moon appears,
glistening, smeared with blood. The husband,
summoned down there by the nurse, who's touched by his
mindless devotion, watches it wax and
wane (but only partway back) behind those
straining purple lips. "Oh god," he

moans, "It's here! It's here!" Well, not quite yet. A
grey-beard doctor arrives on the scene and
takes command (no one's sure who called him)
from the nurse's relinquished position
crouched between the mother's knees, alert as a
quarterback awaiting the snap. A
sizeable village has passed through his hands, but he's still
eager to welcome each new arrival.
The husband watching over his shoulder, the doctor
says, "A few more pushes," giving

signals the mother neither needs nor wants. The
next wave crumbles something in her;
on the next she feels it giving way a
little more; and next, the dam is
broken open, worlds rush through it, a chaos of
feelings so turbulent they cannot
be distinguished from each other swirls and
floods down every artery and
nerve to the site of the making and out of her with a
great, "Oh, god!" and washes her baby

through the arch and portal, sliding to the
doctor's educated fingers.
Next thing the husband knows, the nurse is handing
him a pair of scissors and pointing
where to cut. He hesitates just barely
long enough for me to put my
hand in his and feel the strangely tough and
rubbery umbilicus –
shiny, red, blue-veined – resist his steel.
Perhaps he glimpses the thing I see.

The cord we only seem to have severed entwines
unbroken with countless others to form
the ruddy trunk and branches of a tree,
the forest's tallest, and each strand passes
through the bodies of women, and from these nodes

men hang like leaves. A firmament
of ornaments festoons the upper branches,
our little room among them. I am
clinging to this vision like fall's last apple
resists the drop. The room is clearing.

The gray-beard doctor, gathering purpose about him
like a cloak, hurries off.
The mother surrenders the baby to an aide, who
disappears with it. Then she's helped to a
wheelchair the father slowly pushes away,
both of them smiling, wet-faced, and drained.
From these tears you could grow flowers. The nurse,
ending her shift at last, follows
close behind, and, passing through the door,
notices that her feet don't hurt.

Canto II: Dressing for the Occasion

"Unto us a child is given," I say.
"The rest is commentary. Go study,"
ripostes Dante. He opens the birthing chamber
door with his left hand. His right hand's
sweeping gesture ushers me through to the hallway's
startlingly brilliantly shining floor,
which my feet touch as gently as falling
soap bubbles. I'm barely allowed a
moment of wonder before he conducts me into a
harsh-lit room with sinks, and mirrors

reflecting the battered toilet stalls behind us like
paintings made surreal by what is
left out – me: I'm absent, though I'm there,
figured in furious brushstrokes of grime and
rags he now strips from me, saying, "Don't worry.
No one who comes in here will see you."
Then, with paper towels tepidly moistened and
jets of liquid hand soap, he dabs the
awful accretions off my body, gently and
thoroughly as the nurses dried the

baby half an hour ago. As he's
tying a hospital johnny around me, the

tatters he tossed in the corner shift and rustle.
A scrawny rat emerges from them.
Dante pounces, grabs its tail and swings it
"thock!" against the wall. "Did you
collect a souvenir in hell?" he asks, the
corpse dangling from his hand.
I nod, and confess, "An oven mitt." He smiles.
"Even the finest wool of Satan,

once you bring it here, is merely verminous."
Into the trash goes my purloined keepsake, and
to the wall goes Dante; he passes through it,
just like that, a cloud through a sieve.
Then the door swings open, pushed by him, and
into the hall he beckons me,
cleaned and refreshed and increasingly mystified.
"Can I do that, too?" I ask, "that
walking through walls thing?" "Yes and no," replies my
mentor, "I commend your prudence,

asking for knowledge you more painfully might have
gathered by your own devices.
On this stage of your journey, pedagogical
reasons you may understand – but
only after the lesson has been learned –
counsel loosening all the ties that
straitjacket you within that organism
you are used to suppose is you. The

change was wrought there in the tunnel from hell, while
you were preoccupied, distracted.

Thus, in this attenuated state, that
part of you retaining awareness
floated to the birthing-room floor, slow to
respond to gravity's grip; and less than the
sun's full spectrum and power will not suffice to
illumine you to mortal eyes.
Walk through walls? Oh yes, you might; and
you might waste this tutelage, like
Caliban, whose only profit by the
gift of speech was he could swear.

Beware the thrill of incorporeal fribbles!
Victoria won't be found in them, and the
time you have to find her will be lost.
But, of course, you have free will."
Through the labyrinthine building he leads me,
motivated and mystified.
Each time we arrive at double doors with
high-set reinforced glass windows (the
corridors have more segments than a millipede),
quick as light he vapors through them,

scouts ahead, and cracks them open for me.
So I slip through almost normally,
this time just as the door bursts open and grey-beard

doctor, muttering, hurrying home,
charges through me like a bullet through smoke.
It is the most shocking violation.
It calls me back to an earlier chaos, under
an iron gate; and also a flavor,
the sweet forgetfulness of orgasm; and
the loss of one whose body eclipsed

the world, as his slides past and mine swirls.
He notices our conjunction less
than if I'd been a smell in the hall, an instant's
shudder is all, the kind my father
called in yiddish a "skookh", in English "somebody
stepped on your grave." Dante says,
"People can do that to you. It's different,
doing it and having it done."
He holds the door. My mouth still warm with the taste
of the doctor's anticipated cigar,

I hang back a moment, then sidle on through.
We walk far. Sometimes the corridors'
walls are yellow, sometimes chewed-kale green.
Clusters of nurses chat at their stations.
Bored men bulling buffers about remove the
scuffs and skids and scratches the weight of the
day bore into these floors. Our footsteps don't echo.
Each of the rooms that line each side of the
halls through which we are a moving absence

contains its own, particular suffering.

Somehow it is known to me. There, a
woman floats in a coma. Cancer
shipwrecked her. Voices come to her pure and distant as
sea-birds' cries. Her husband, sleeping
in the chair beside her bed, her life raft,
is not ready to let her go.
He will wake to the feeling it is he who
bobs on the deep, clutching the gunwale.
So, the waves caressing her cheekbones, she
allows her lungs to inflate and buoy her

towards the shore that only he will reach.
Halls and halls and halls - Dante
pulls me away in haste each time I stop. At
last, we exit a modest metal
door in the rear of the building. Lock and alarm
arrangements give way to Dante. I pause on the
stoop and look behind me. There's a placard,
Office of Medical Examiner –
Authorized Personnel Only. "That's the morgue,"
I say, "But I don't remember passing

through the place they keep the bodies. I think that
I would remember something like that!"
"Our business for now is with the living," he answers.
I say, "Okay, but when do we climb

the Mountain of Purgatory? Isn't that where
we'll meet Victoria? At the top?"
"This is the City of Purgatory. Remember,
now it's your world, no longer mine.
You, who scrape the tops off mountains for coal,
who fill the valleys with garbage, who scrape the

meadows level for parking, who fill the marshes with
concrete and pylons, who build and tear down,
who level the high places and raise the low, have
flattened Purgatory. Now the
eminence that was lit when your lives were dark
is worn away, by you! And you
have grown your city upon and with its rubble.
It rises no higher than your living
feet can walk. You've been to the Champ de Mars,
Tienanmen, the Federal Quadrangle?

In a place like those, we'll find her. She waits."
Again he sets off, and I follow.
As within, so without. A maze of
paths twines the hospital complex,
asphalt on lawns blue-grey in the moonlight, the moonlight
pock-marked by halogen lamps, the paths like
streams connecting featureless parking lot lakes,
here and there a solitary
car like a boat moored for the night, the stars.
We come to a grassy quarter-acre

dotted with marble benches and waist-high shrubs,
sloping down to a broad embankment and
six now quiet lanes of tan concrete;
half a dozen birch trees streak the
dimmest, farthest, lower corner; beneath them, a
dozen pale and wavering shapes like
photographic negatives of shadows
blotch the dark. My guide leads me
among them, men and women in size and form,
but featureless. They make welcoming noises.

Canto III – The Excommunicated

"But this one has a tether!" says one, pointing
at my abdomen with a hand as
shaky as moonbeams on a rippling pond.
Whatever he or she may see there,
I can't. "Yes," says Dante, "he remains
bound up with his remains," and explains
my status as a "visitor" and our mission.
"Ooooh" and "aaah" they intone. "Now go," says
Dante, with a dismissive flick of the wrist, "You've
miles to go before you sleep."

They disperse into the darkness. I ask,
"Who are they?" He says, "They're just the
sort of thing you might have expected. I must
leave you now. But you may meet me at
sundown at the Presidential Library." He
spreads his arms as if to hug me;
I step forward, eager to hold him long
enough to feel grounded in his love; and
at that moment, the sun's first rays land on my
back; my shadow pierces him; and

I am alone, above the highway, among the
birches, in my hospital johnny,

listening to the birds' dawn cries, the soft, warm
air on my skin reminding me how
open my garment, how exposed I am.
I retreat at once across a
driveway, off the hospital grounds, into the
sumac and unruly grasses, the
weather-bleached litter, the weedy privacy, there to
kneel unseen and consider my options.

Finding her, of course, is the only option,
now that she's sent for me, a third of a
century after her death. I cry for her,
crouched among dandelions and thistles:
for her, to her, not sure which it is or
if these tears will wash us closer.
Maybe it's a purely bodily function.
Maybe it's a form of prayer.
Can it truly be both? Here, where the sun that
illuminates, obnubilates.

If I were to turn aside, and bring back
to my former life the knowledge
that I might have found her but chose not to,
how am I to live that life
any less unchanged than if I were to
follow this path to its end and
find her standing there, thigh muscles swelling,
teeth glistening in a smile? I

bring her back each way: the one, as a torment
familiar but infinitely heightened;

or, as whatever wonders may become when
they take root in the dirt of the real.
I wish I could say a resolute wave of emotion
lifts me now to seek her forth, but
really it is my body, that brings to mind with
muscle cramps and pins and needles
how whole-heartedly unhappy it is at
staying so long so still and unflexing.
I get up, stretch and rub the knots, and absently
follow a little path beneath the

flaming sumac spears, above the highway
some small distance. The thicket thins and
dwindles, and human voices reach into it from
just ahead. I halt, and spy through the
scanty veil of leaves an overpass bridge that
shelters the talkers; and wanting not to
be caught lurking, I step into the sunlight.
Taking no notice of my approach, they
lie companionably on sheets of cardboard
on a level strip of dirt. Their

only wall, the bridge's concrete abutment, is
decorated with swirling graffiti. The
man with the weathered, round, red face and mat of

hair as coarse and tan as jute,
continues his story: "There's a place the freights
slow down around a bend. It's flat there,
nothing but yellow grass and red-tailed hawks.
Awful quiet. You can hear them
come a long ways off. You miss your train,
you'll wait tomorrow for the next one

going north, and maybe you'll see a pickup
truck pass by in all that time, and
maybe you won't. I was there a couple
hours, the tracks commenced to hum.
By the grade's this big old junction box that
I was sitting behind, and I had
plenty of time to get awake and ready to
make my move. They were slowing
with the engines, didn't hardly brake,
but just a little, sshhh! Sshhh!

I come round the side of the box and just
about to run across when twenty
Mexicans rose from the ground, mamas and papas and
little kids – I hadn't seen or
heard a peep the whole time I was there – and
made for the boxcar I'd picked out. Well...
I just stood there with my mouth hung open.
Almost made me miss my ride."
Now he turns his eyes on me and asks me,

"What can I do for you, friend?"

I say, "That reminds me how they used to
excommunicate all sorts of
people, but that didn't keep them out of
heaven." There's a land, far off, where
people have no neck and one eye in the
middle of the chest and speak in
purest gibberish. Perhaps I've recently
come from there. Perhaps they have.
They wait, polite as if I've said hello, for
me to reveal if I'll make sense, and

if so, what sort. So, I plunge ahead:
"Do you know where a person might find some
regular clothes - for free?" Holding my hands at my
sides, palms open, head cocked, as if to
say this stupid johnny is all I've got.
"The Sally Army's down that way, but
you don't look like you need nothing. What, you
want a three piece suit? Heh heh. They
call me Alabama," he says, extending a
hand. We shake. I look down, flustered.

Canto IV – The Tardy to Waken

I stare at my feet splayed in the dirt and
at the columns that rise from them,
swelling gracefully around the calves but knobby
at the knees the gown's blue drapery
hangs to, almost, and say, "You're sure I look like...
everything's there... clothing-wise...."
And now a pause. I'm making them uneasy.
Although they're used to the strangest of strangers,
they also are used to being on their guard.
Alabama's friend sits up, says,

"Shirt... shorts... shoes... you got it all, mate."
Bracing himself to fight, if he has to.
He does it a lot, gets beaten a lot, his face
is marked. Its what he's used to. It scares
away the ones who are not. It doesn't bother
me that I know this. Only now,
telling you, does it seem strange. I say,
"Okay. Well, thanks." I move my feet
as if to go, but Alabama reads me
better than his friend did: "Don't you

mind him. Are you missing something, brother?
I don't think I caught your name."

I suppress the urge to say I'm Clarence,
Angel Second Class. "Seth.
I guess your friend is right. I've got it all."
Smiling brightly, I turn away to
where the earth banks sharply to the road.
For a while now, morning birdsong has
been drowned out by morning commuters' metal
grinding in oil, gas exploding, and

rubber abrading on asphalt. From above,
I watch them hurry, strapped in their cages.
A woman who ordered her daughter aboard this morning's
schoolbus despite yesterday's fever
leadfoots her way to work as if to bring the
day's end closer, faster. A man, hunched forward,
grips the wheel as if to escape the back seat
passengers. They ignore him, excitedly
waving their arms over last night's baseball games.
Nearby, his best friend's wife is dying.

Encased like a fish in a glass and metal tank,
a man steers and applies the gas,
as though he weren't hip-deep in the Neversink,
plying a carbide wand, the trout line's
perfect curlicue hissing overhead. A
man thinks over and over, if Bush were to
cross the road here I'd forget how to work the
brakes. Worried that she'll be late, a

woman talks intently on her cell phone to
someone who makes her feel less alone.

A man is annoyed by this big-assed pickup truck
he can't see over or around
and all the other things that block his view.
A man is anxious he'll be late.
And another. And a woman. And a
string of them, anxious; anxiety tinged with
anger or nibbled by fear or just barely controlled or
writhing like a restless sleeper
in the pit of this man's stomach. He punches his
radio's scan button every time it

settles on a station. There's a trucker
pondering where she'll be at lunch time.
And, boxed in behind the eighteen wheeler, a
ton and a half of SUV to his
left (the driver's wondering did he leave the
stove turned on) and two blue tons of
SUV to his right (the driver's regretting
what she did with her hair) and a hungover
twenty-year-old in a bread truck close behind, a
man sits upright on a Harley,

delicately flexing his wrist on the throttle,
serene, alert, air-stroked, and smiling to
feel his tires caress the grain of the road.

All except for him presume that
they are safe between the yellow dashes,
sealed in metal lozenges hurtling
to their dooms obscured in clouds of thought.
Alabama says, "They call it
going to work." "That's right," his friend affirms. I
tell them the name of the place I'm supposed to

find by sundown. They've not heard of it. But
Alabama says, "It's probly
downtown, be my guess. I'll get you started
that way. Headed there myself, you
want to tag along. You comin', Billy?"
Billy looks down and grumbles no: he's
got a can of beans that he can eat; he's
happy he won't have to share them.
Watching Alabama, I'm not sure how
much of this is spoken, how much

simply understood. I'm dizzy, a moment.
Selfish bastard – my thought – clashes
in my head with Alabama's amused
sadness. Then he's standing, climbing the
weedy shoulder to the overpass. I
have to scramble to catch up,
leaving Billy below us full of sourness,
like he'd eaten the beans already.
Soon I'm once again upon a bridge

above a channel full of humans –

unlike the brutal or shattered structures I have
crossed so recently, this arch is
graceful as the small of a woman's back.
Winding out of sight behind us, a
green and leafy avenue. Ahead, a
street lined with storefronts and three-story houses
arrows straight into the haze the city's
million iron lungs create when they
breathe. Plate-glass windows reflect a bleary
glare onto nearly empty sidewalks.

Figures appear, blocks away, and vanish
into buildings or onto side streets, or
walk the way we're going, pulling away. We
don't walk fast. It's hot and humid, a
sheen of sweat on Alabama's forehead.
His gait's a relaxed, slow-motion lope.
We don't talk much. I think of asking him
this city's name, no stranger a question
than some ones I've asked already, just to
hear what he would say. *I killed a*

man in Reno, just to watch him die, sings
Johnny Cash, somewhere, lamenting
idle curiosity, perhaps.
Whatever he'd say, it's Purgatory.

Slouching beside me, he holds within him, swaddled in
feelings of protective kinship
with the bumbling and foolish, some unreadable
wish for something in return, but
I cannot see what, it glints like something that
may be a fish or leaves or old iron

veiled in murky currents on a stream bed. He
stops at a storefront, says, "You keep on
straight, maybe you'll hit it. Or… I got
enough for a pint of rose in here.
You throw in a buck, and we could make it a quart."
"Sorry." "Okay. So long, then, pilgrim."
He stands and watches me go with the same sadness
he had watching Billy, clutching
his amusement like a rail to keep from
falling in, then turns to the store.

Canto V – The Lately Repentant

About a hundred yards ahead, beneath
a sky the color of watery milk,
the street's sparse traffic slows and clots. Police
cars, parked where no one normally parks,
occlude the lane, their occupants dark and still,
their flashers beating at the front
of what might be the oldest house this otherwise
shabbily newish neighborhood
can boast: three stories, brick, its gingerbread trim
and porches glossy, sensible brown,

slate mansard roof, unweathered plywood
panels neatly fitted in the
first floor window frames, set back from the street,
its yard a patch of dirt some grass
as thin as hairs on a balding head the shade
of a gnarly crabapple tree whose crown
a dust-drab blur I spied from blocks away:
flanked by modern wood-frame boxes,
among their dull geometry a darker
lozenge pulsing acid blue.

Also blocks away I felt the heat.
Between the cops and the house, the sidewalk

bears a line of several dozen people.
Holding hands, a greybeard and his
grey-haired wife. A twenty-something mother
hoists her weary-eyed, thumb-sucking
toddler shoulder high. A middle-aged woman
sips a coffee, passes the cup towards
forty years of alpha malehood; but he
waves it off (his other neighbor

looks on wistfully) and waggles his sign, a
color cartoon of a fetus
coiled in utero, at motorists who
resolutely stare ahead,
preferring the less disturbing glow of brake lights.
In him burns a sullen frustration.
I can see it – can they, too? – an azure
cone of flame, a pilot light. I
see it with a sense beside the senses
or composed of them oddly combined.

Suddenly he and his comrades flare like a bank of
jets on a gas grill turned to char,
bright and pale as a cloudless noon-time zenith.
What has triggered this eruption
and sustains it, predatory, tense, is
not at first apparent. The cops roll
lazily out of their cruisers and saunter over
to a small green car that's stopped at the

curb between them. When they reach its bumpers, the
passenger door cracks open just

enough for a skinny, eighteen-year-old girl
to slip through, hurried, eyes cast down.
The door snicks shut behind her as the cops
close in, a burly man each side.
The line on the sidewalk divides in two. Its halves
collapse into clusters that draw apart
just enough to leave a path for the cops
and the girl they buffer between them, but not
quite fast enough for Officer Moon, who chides
a laggard, "Move it, lady, you

know the injunction says no interference."
"Bless you," she says, and steps aside.
"Honey," she says, "Please don't kill your baby."
What she thinks she is feeling, she would
like to label "love," this mixture of stage fright,
sentimental fantasy (the
infant pink and mild), and iron compulsion to
bear her witness into the world. A
few nearby are praying audibly. A
man with a ball of anger in his

chest looks for the best place to throw it.
I can hear the burners hiss.
The girl between the cops shrinks into herself

like rising dough that's been punched down.
Officer Moon, holds her left arm.
They have almost reached the door, when a
light strikes upon them so pure and intense it
fades the rest to insignificance.
She's a year or two younger than the one who
carries the object of all their attention,

a girl with brown hair tied back tight beneath
a scarf (she thinks it's "mousy"), wearing
peasant blouse and jeans, who stands out like a
virid flame in a rank of blue, whose
passion is focused through her tears just as a
lighthouse beacon through its lens; she
burns with hormonal power and anguish at "murder"
sanctioned by "the law and its minions."
So the words beat behind her eyes. She
came here over her mother's objections.

The clinic door opens, and the escorts
unhand their charge, who enters as if
pushed from behind. The crowd subsides, except for
the girl in the peasant blouse, who torments
herself – imagine what's going on inside.
Armored in boredom, Officer Moon,
returning to his cruiser, heralds the billionth
second of his earthly existence by
clearing his throat. It passes. I watch it float by

like a soap bubble on this now much

gentler air. The line reforms on the sidewalk with
only a few incandescences.
Minor concerns of being assert themselves:
an itchy crotch surreptitiously scratched,
a thirst relieved, a glance at a watch, a quiet
comparing of what it has been like to
be here, defining and taming what it's been like –
the weaving of verbal baskets around
the crickets they hope experience will turn into.
The man hoists his cartoon fetus.

Could this be what I was meant to see?
I listen to their chirping voices.
Could this be what I was meant to hear?
Should I linger, or head downtown?
The clinic door opens. A woman strides
onto the porch, surveying the crowd and the
delicate latticework of cages splintered by
crickets turning into dragons.
Officer Moon and his colleague sip and return their
cups of coffee to their dashboards.

Pausing, she places one hand on the rail, to connect with
something firm. Her gaze holds steady,
blue-eyed, sharp as a sword, tempered in anguish.
She straightens her spine. It looks like a shiver.

Then, resolved to walk right through them, looking them
down, she descends the four steps – clop
clop clop clop. Traffic noises
suddenly seem far away.
Of all these people – the cops, now warily tense;
the men now clutching their signs like clubs;

the mothers drawing their kids to them; their prayers
like smokestacks venting whatever's in them;
all of them focused as one on this approaching
body, empty and alone,
slight in her modest green suit – only I,
drawn to stand so near the crowd she
counts me, when her gaze flicks past, among their
number (it stings), am here to witness:
her blade's tip pierces the tongue of flame
the girl in the peasant blouse shoots at her.

In the shock, a moment of clarity locks them.
In the girl the woman sees
herself, a younger avatar in a series
flipping past like a deck of cards
that begins and ends with a joker. A sob
bloats her throat and nearly escapes. The
girl sees herself, and the girl who stood where she stands an
instant ago is consumed and gone.
Not even smoke marks the extinguishment; but,
it will be years before she knows.

The day that follows the kali yuga is
the same as the day that went before,
as it is said. For now, she is troubled and distant.
The woman who thinks she is filled with love says
"Honey, we will surely pray for you,"
words utterly wasted on both the
vanquished combatants. The woman in the green suit
breaks through the line and marches away,
looking to neither side, eyes filled with the blankness of
youth, the brightness of all that we lose.

Canto VI: In the Clouds

After that, to hang around seems pointless.
Officer Moon, as I walk by him,
greets his one billion one thousandth second of life with a
hearty yawn. His watchful cop's eyes
take me in and quickly release me: "bum."
Afraid of contact, I sidle past the
burning Christians half-unnoticed, the subject
of some other week's sermon.
Shall I pause and speak to the peasant blouse girl?
What could I express to her?

Perhaps that vicarious intimacy we feel
for those we've beheld being touched by others,
perhaps that she reminds me of Victoria
without being anything like her but young.
The sidewalk stretches straight into the haze.
Soon I am alone on it, and
soon can't see my feet for the cloudy cocoon of
thought I've woven all around me.
Its burden, if a cloud may be said to bear one,
is the efficacy of prayer.

They march around calling down the light on others
like spotters calling in an air strike.

Despite the fervor boiling in their skulls,
nothing answers. Despite their persistent
invocation of divine interference
with these purposes, these bricks,
the house continues to stand uncauterized of
its business, its clients to come and go.
And yet, if a prayer is a query addressed beyond
our power, perhaps the peasant-bloused virgin's

sparked a rejoinder? A storm of millivolts
behind her eyes, a similar storm
approaching, never touching: what leaped between them,
ineludibly piercing and swift,
unwilled, unwilling, fixing them each in each other's
memory as unfading as the
shadows imprinted on Hiroshima's pavements?
For this, of course, no deity's needed.
Like a gentle bell, the thought of silent
godless prayer awakens me.

Discs of shadow dot the broken concrete
sidewalk every fifty feet for
blocks ahead, identical as the Norway
maples that cast them; half the day done.
Where am I going? When will I get there? Will I
want to eat or sleep on the way?
Casting back my head and peering up, I
ask the ferocious solar blob to

give me a sign, but in this neighborhood
there's not much signage and none of it's helpful.

Gaily painted, tight-packed triple-deckers
line the lane like books on a shelf
about as far as pollution permits me to see.
I pause for a moment's probosculation.
Across a shallow yard's weeds and half-filled
inflatable wading pool, a very
fat old woman dozes on her porch,
slumped in her wicker chair, arms crossed.
Curled on the shelf of her bosom a tabby cat sleeps,
riding peaceful respirations.

Telling you of this brings it back to me as
if I were standing there! – and after
not too many heartbeats thinking this:
*The sight of these two mammals enjoying so
fully the little they have in common should shame you to
weeping, America!* How hard can it
be to care for one another? Your rich
begrudge your poor their mite. Your poor
begrudge each other. The ones in the middle fear
the ones below them, bend the knee to the

moneyed, and keep an eye on their neighbors. The space a
dollar takes is more than you would
spare the creatures around you. You're free with this:

you shit your nest and everywhere else. You
stomp around the world with an anxious smile and a
big knife, taking whatever you
want, and whoever gets in your way had better
look to god for help. You wonder
why they hate you, who cried your name with longing,
back in the days of FDR.

Your bodies, your selves, your world, awareness touches
glancingly, as if its business makes
other, more pressing demands. So disconnected, you
float in faith's warm bath. The bulk of
life slides dreamily by. You wallow in stuff. One
flawless morning your tallest buildings
vanish in a puff of smoke. Your president,
turning havoc to his own ends,
wreaks it mightily in your name. "Meanwhile," he
counsels you, "Go shopping". You do.

Later, you look up from the pricetags you study as
if your lives were written there to
applaud his boast a mission's been accomplished.
Then, feeling safer, you return to
choosing among the fruits of foreign sweatshops. The
Terror Alert level holds at "orange".
So, as easy as shooting a friend in the face, the
rhythm's established: shopping and fear and
shopping and fear and church and shopping and fear; and

when it's time, you cheer him on to

Baghdad and the murder of the innocents.
A few days after I stand before the
snoozing lady and her cat, a Storm will
drown your beautiful southernmost port,
changing its streets into swimming pools, its attics
into suffocation chambers.
Soon as it's safe, he'll stand in the floodlit, sodden
square and make fine promises like an
actor playing a TV politician. It
doesn't matter what he says. The

mission's accomplished. "What mission?" you might ask, but
you didn't ask when it would have mattered.
Perhaps, in view of our manifest unfitness, the
clearest evidence we are likely to
get of a loving god's existence is our
continued presence on the earth.
Some six hundred seventy years ago, Ambrogio
Lorenzetti anticipated
Capra's *It's a Wonderful Life* by painting
the walls of the hall where Siena's elite

did their republic's business with lovely frescoes
showing their town and its hilly countryside
governed, here, quite well, and there, quite poorly.
You, Vermont, so justly proud of your

politics almost as clear and deep blue as the
sky where Ambrogio's brush suspended his
bodiless spirits of stable republican virtue,
look: can you see yourself in the ring dance the
women weave on the cobblestones next to the merchants'
peaceful stalls? A man buys shoes. The

dancers and singers excite no comment among the
many but not too many who pass on
foot and horseback with calm and friendly smiles, the
well-to-do better dressed than the rest but
not by much, unarmed. The streets are clean, the
buildings well maintained, and well fed
peasants, decently clad, send laden donkeys
into town from orderly fields. Or
is the city of crumbling buildings your mirror?
Barefoot people walk past the cobbler's and

past the bodies lying in the street. The
rich stay hidden and carry weapons.
Clots of people hang around the square and
quarrel. Drunks drop junk from towers. The
Totentanz of armored men is all that
ventures across the blackened pastures.
You might say, not much like Chittenden County, where
no one is homeless, the shelters and food shelf
are as empty as the prisons, and never a
meadow lost its flowers for Walmart; so

far from Newport, where none of Main Street's windows is
boarded, and cheerful natives find plenty of
interesting work; another world from Spear Street's
McMansions and Essex County's trailers. Your
Democrats and Progressives can tell you, no faction
trumps the common good. Your governor
keeps your National Guard at home, to serve you.
Seek your face in Ambrogio's fresco. And
know that eight years later he died of the plague that
took half his city's people.

Canto VII: Close Encounters

She unshutters her eyes, and her fixed focus
shows that she's been watching me through
slitted lids. I feel like a dragonfly under
consideration by a not so
hungry frog. Pursing her lips, she croaks,
"What are you staring at, young man?"
"Sorry. I was thinking, just happened to stop in
front of your house. I'll move along, now."
"Khrrarrh." She clears her throat, and now her voice is
honey sprinkled with rust, melodious.

"My old man - may he rest in peace - was that way, a
passing thought could take him" a wave of the
hand, like flicking water. "Used to make me mad!" but
now, the thought of it casts a circle of
golden radiance almost as far as me. "I'm
sorry to hear he's gone," I say, and
venture a toe into the spotlight. "Sounds like
he was quite a guy. I bet you
miss him very much." It flickers, then steadies.
"Well, he passed so long ago." The

spotlight's moved a couple of inches, left me
barely toeing the rim. Should I

follow? Closer and closer is how that goes, and
who knows how long I'll be trapped, with
who knows how far still to go before nightfall.
Bargain. "Maybe you could help me?
How would I get to the Presidential Library?"
Long, slow blink. "Now why would you want to
read about a bunch of politicians?"
Slaps her knee and grins. I'm sure I

look like no-one's image of a scholar.
"Meeting a friend there," I say, and something
must have ignited in my voice to make it
cast its own lights and shadows.
Dropping her banter, she looks at me and says, "We
don't have anything like that here; but
that way there's a park. It might be there."
Leans her head back, shuts her eyes. The
cat, which raised its head when she slapped her knee,
burrows its nose back into its rib cage.

Her spotlight irises shut. I tarry a while,
as if alone on a darkened stage
awaiting the curtain's drop to close the act;
but I could swear, as I walk off
I feel her eyes on my back to the end of the block.
Then I cross the street and there's nothing.
Across the street, there's only the afternoon's
muggy heat riding my shoulders.

I trudge some miles through sour little thoughts:
I handled her badly. I should have held

*myself in check and listened ingratiatingly
to that selfish bitch who knows more
than she said – I'm sure of it! – but cannot
stand to share the stage. Except with her
stupid sleepy mangy cat. She couldn't have
cut me off quicker with a machete.
Fucked it up,* I did. And on and on, these
otiose, corrosive broodings,
monotonous as pavement and humid heat,
condense and trickle in my skull, a

kind of mist that even in the bludgeoning
glare of an August afternoon seems
characteristic of this place. *Hell, by
contrast, though murky, seemed clear. The shock of
constant surprise and fear made it seem that way,
perhaps. A meditation teacher
startles you by shouting "phat!" and that is the
moment of wakeful enlightenment.* And
on and on, anon, one step at a time, I
trudge through gaps in the swirling mist.

Helios' chariot, which science teaches
won't be hijacked by Phaëton for several
billion years, has sloped halfway from its zenith to

where the horizon would be if it wasn't
obscured by buildings whose shadows mitigate the
afternoon's mugginess, when to the
right the promised green space suddenly opens.
A couple of circuits around its perimeter
proves conclusively there's no library here.
The sun is squatting on the rooftops.

It's nearly evening, the appointed hour,
and I've nowhere to go. I slouch on a
bench made of recycled milk bottles molded to look like
planks of shit-brown plastic "wood."
Have you ever felt, at the end of a day of
slogging work, your muscles relax, and
with that something drains like hourglass sand,
only it's draining from your head, and
suddenly you can see your world again?
So the view from my bench restores me.

Aah. And consider: most of a monkey's attention is
lavished on other monkeys. Why should
I be different? The park is sprinkled with people.
There are a father and son, and the ball that
passes between them traces strands of a cable
thick as the ones that hold up bridges.
There a man in a hat reads a paper, muttering.
There an old woman walks a puppy.
The man in the hat is not happy about the puppy.

The old woman knows, but doesn't care.

A circle of six erects an invisible structure of
rules and flings a frisbee in it.
The frisbee breaks the rules and lands at my feet.
I toss it back. A boy and a girl
lollygagging beyond the raucous playground,
about the age we were when last
I and Victoria saw each other, shoot
gossamer strands stronger than steel
floating like milkweed towards each other's future.
It's bitter, not to see her again;

but, how shall I find her, if I've lost my guide?
It's bitter, to wander misdirected.
I sit with my bitterness on the bench, two friends.
Perhaps I shall wander the earth like Elijah.
In the diminishing light, the people gather
their ethereal webs like fishermen
rolling nets for stowage, and head back to the
comforts of their defining boxes.
The last to leave are the laughing six, but not
until their frisbee's glowing green.

To my eyes, it leaves a verdant trail that
intersects lines that moonlight draws on
signs and lamp posts and tree branches' imperfect arches,
defining planes that hang among them;

planes that growing night solidifies; its
velvety tint grows thicker than a
frisbee's traces; rooms of night surround me,
nocturno-classical columns and plinths, a
frieze of politicians. I rise and enter the
Presidential Library.

Canto VIII: Delinquent Leaders

Along about dawn, I dream two angels fight
in pantomime with golden swords
on stage. The house is packed with all of us,
and as each blow, elaborately
flourished, snakes across the air, it snicks
some of the spectators' heads clean off.
Yet, people compete to seize their seats. I'm dragged
along towards the front. Then I'm awake.
Someone has thoughtfully draped a newspaper on me,
on my bench. And now I remember

last night in the Library. My guide,
encircled by his pale flock,
met me in the foyer. "You are late,"
he called. "I got here as soon as I could,"
I said, "which is to say I'd given up thinking
I'd get here at all, and here I was."
"My son," he replied, "you think so much to remarkably
little effect. But here you are."
Then, stepping through the stationary circle –
a poplar escaping a fairy ring –

he led me hallway by hallway to the room
where presidents are collected, a spacious

marmoreal cube. There Jefferson weeps for his slaves,
and Kennedy for the Bay of Pigs,
and Reagan for that turbulent priest Romero,
the slaughtered nuns and campesinos.
In unpowered wheelchairs, they remorse.
"Amputated at the knee, the
limbs each left in hell," said Dante. On the
Gipper's shoulder, McKinley laid a

compassionate hand, then walked away from him.
A tall man, facing away from me,
strode to McKinley. I think it was that other
reluctant warrior, LBJ,
who hugged him with horribly truncated arms, that ended
above the wrists; in this, like Nixon,
who crouched alone in a corner, sobbing the full-throated
sobs of one who has broken loose,
drawing from the others occasional glances of
brotherhood, affection, and grief.

Into this atmosphere of dignified sorrow
(except for Nixon, who was never
more himself than when he was being awkward)
broke a shrill, squeaking, piping,
unpleasant voice. It came from a man who sprawled
his extravagant length on an Eames chair. His face
reminded me of felling trees with an axe.
Cutting a vee, the curved blade chips a

deepening series of concavities. His
cheeks, his temples, the sockets under his

brows looked carved that way; and, judging by his
deep grey eyes, suffering did it.
"Gentlemen, we have visitors," he drawled, and
rose to meet us, lanky and towering.
Winding his way through several dozen former
chief executives, he paused for
numerous greetings, stooping to a hug or a
kiss in the hollows of his face, and he
gave as good as he got. I noted how gently he
repositioned armless Harry

Truman's wheelchair out of his path. We silently
waited for him, and when he reached us
he smiled a smile of simple happiness
above which rode those comfortless eyes
so for that moment his face contained all humanity.
Dante talked; I couldn't speak.
"Good sir, descending from that serene state
where both my being and your nature's
better angels reside, the other side of the
valley of error I met my companion. He

hales from those Green Mountains whose sons so dearly
and with such distinction hallowed
Cedar Creek and Cemetery Ridge.

But he will see the morning sun.
I bring him at the behest of a lady whose love
for him perturbs her tranquility
as water troubles water." "Have we met?
I do believe we have, though I
cannot recall it now. You find me lowered
in my spirits. You're passing through?

I'm pleased to meet you. Tell me – I thirst to hear it –
how do you find the Republic fares?"
This last was addressed to me, the rest to Dante.
He asked as if knowing was all he wanted.
Who could refuse? I said, "It seems that Franklin's
doubts as to whether we could keep it are
proving too well founded." "The Republic
Franklin gave us and the one that
I passed on to you are different things.
The one was stuck together with laws,

the other is bound by sacrifice and blood.
In that sense Franklin's doubts are true."
"And now we are fettered by hatred and fear," I said,
and, pained to see how much this pained him,
added, "You and my guide may have met in some finer
dimension I have yet to visit,
but I've met you without your meeting me.
In a three-walled white stone shelter
(I wish they'd used some black granite blocks),

your statue sits brooding upon the open;

into the walls above it are carved the words in
which you showed us your devotion."
"That was erected just before Mr. Wilson –
he's over there – filled the bag of
shadows that detains him here. Each one of us
possesses a bag that he must empty
before he may retire to the sunny fields
your friend inhabits. I'm sorry to tell you,
it's not as easy as drowning a sack of kittens."
He paused. I waited, then asked what he meant.

He thought, and asked if I had served as a soldier.
"I didn't have no quarrel with them
Viet Congs." He said, "Did not Ali say
also that no Viet Cong
ever called him 'nigger'? What could you say
that might ache with such a sting?"
"Honest Abe," I said, "when I was at that
age where young men, believing in their
immortality, seek something to die for,
my country offered me nonsense and lies."

He said, "Then maybe you will understand
a part at least of what I tell you.
There is something that a man who's sighted
another man along a rifle's

barrel knows, that you can only imagine.
You chose a different conception of manhood.
Some of us are tempered by the fires of
conscience and of battle; but, others
avoid looking maturity in the eye
until too late, it's looked away.

Those overgrown boys for whom Iraq now suffers
are fighting the shadows of all they failed
to choose. A man like that's a pig in a poke.
He's hidden inside his packaging. When
you tear away the bows and ribbons, you
may count on finding something smaller
and meaner than what you might have been led to expect.
So one man walks around wrapped in shadows,
and one man carries his shadows in a bag.
I will tell you what's in mine.

Some of it, anyways. I was so blessed
clever, I worked so dreadfully hard,
I sweated out with such excruciating
patience those long weeks to be
assured that they not we would fire first
across the harbor at Sumter and
the odium of aggressor would fall to them
together with that hapless fort.
Such morality comes to seem a small, a
very small thing indeed, when

faced with the judgments of the Lord pronounced in
syllables of corpses, paragraphs of
hecatombs, inscrutable, silent, and final.
Should I have let the South secede?
Here, where we have laid all burdens down
except that one, invisible
to you, of which I'm speaking, no one cares.
That burden: the weight a body brings
into the world by leaving, multiplied
by every breath it might have breathed

and soul it might have touched but for the fact
of how we chose to live our lives;
each body so affected adds its measure
of respiration and communion
frustrated. Now I draw a breath on behalf of
Private William W. Wickwire,
First Vermont, standing for him as he
might have stood the minute the doctor
told him that his son was born, and so my
load is lessened by the heft of

air in a sigh. It's like unpacking a haywagon
one straw at a time by becoming that
straw and flying away. Perhaps the South's
'Peculiar Institution' would have
sufficed to distinguish its case from others who might have

argued to follow it out of the Union.
Perhaps in a generation or two, the bondsman
would have wiped the sweat from his brow and
seen the way to Zion by lights of his own.
Perhaps he and his former master

would prepare together to greet Katrina and
mark her passing with songs, not dirges."
Here the President coughed and seemed unwilling
or unable to continue.
Dante, at my elbow, said something that sounded like
"find your way by tomorrow's headlines,"
but I barely paid attention: the room
had begun to spin, and I was drawn –
it must have been up, but it seemed like down – into
the darkness welling in Lincoln's eyes.

Canto IX: Follow the Lede

Night has soothed the fine bite of smog in the
back of my throat, for now. Soon day's fresh
load of acids and particulates will
burn and scratch anew. For now, what
chemicals fill the air around my bench are
mainly molecular syllables uttered by
beeches, maples, ashes, oaks and birches, the
vegetable gossip of talkative trees. I'd
like to understand what they are saying,
eavesdrop on the affairs of the rooted.

Weather reports, most likely. Bugs and fire.
Do they broadcast news of us?
Such thoughts carry echoes of last night, his
urgent voice: "tomorrow's headlines."
Suddenly eager – it's a scavenger hunt! – I
sit bolt upright, catch the paper
before it hits the ground, and scan it, hoping
seventy-two point Franklin Gothic
screams her whereabouts, succinctly; hoping
MAN FINDS LOST FIRST LOVE ALIVE.

Instead: **Sergeant First Class Chris J. Chapin,**
pierced through the heart by a sniper's bullet.

The story is written as they always are.
He volunteered, believed in his mission,
and died. The kindly words of friends and family,
copiously quoted, give
no sense of the set of his chin on all those evenings
his own hands lifted off his helmet,
over and over. Of such tales, this war, he's
one thousand eight hundred seventy-fourth.

Bush says "peace mom" wrong about everything.
She wants to meet him face to face,
to have him explain to her why her son died.
"I understand her anguish. I met
with a lot of families. She doesn't represent
the views of a lot of families that
I have met with. And I'll continue to meet with families."
Perhaps the families he meets don't ask,
the story doesn't tell. The past few years,
more Americans are fat,

most numerously in those regions most
inclined to share the President's terror
when he asks them to, and to trust him
to deliver them from evil.
Experts offer a plethora of theories
without mentioning comfort food.
The mother who accused the man who sang
Billie Jean and *In the Closet*

of corruptly touching her son's childhood was
charged with welfare fraud on Tuesday.

Falsely claiming she was indigent, she had
pocketed nineteen thousand dollars.
That same day, fuel prices rising, the
oil men running the country threatened
auto makers that their pickups, mini-
vans and some though not all SU
Vs (but nary a Hummer or passenger car) might
have to get more mpg's in
six years, maybe. Critics are said to be critical.
Business news: big numbers.

Inventories bloated with eight hundred
fifty million dollars worth of
stuff a reckless underling purchased, former
K-Mart Chief Execs pretended
it was merely a seasonal blip, like spring-time's
last wet snows that soon will melt, and
covered up the loss by holding back some
five hundred seventy million dollars
owed to vendors. They are charged with fraud.
Meanwhile, the oil men who run the country

fund their wars off budget, to great applause.
The paper reports a world so strange!
Like Herodotus' tales of the Neuri who turned into

werewolves, the bald Agrippeans, the Lydian
men for whom nakedness was shameful, the women of
Babylon who all were sacred
prostitutes, the Thracians who sent their gods a
message by tossing a man in the air to
fall on upraised javelins – and not a
word of it seems true to life.

Where I live, to witness violent death
stops us where we stand, startled,
frozen in bright jelly, unable to
recall the usual formulas.
Where I live, a dead child's mother's questions
are known to be unanswerable
and sacred, and it is shameful not to look
into her eyes. Where I live,
bodies and souls cannot be measured except
together. Where I live, we don't

enquire too closely what our neighbors do.
Where I live, the dreadful clinch of
money and government hovers as distant and hard to
comprehend as the Milky Way and the
black hole slowly sucking us into its heart,
so obscured by city lights,
colliding stars and all the ephemeral dazzle.
We look up to it only sometimes, on
nights when there's nothing else to do, and sigh, and

say, "How awesome," and say, "How lovely."

I've despaired, almost, of finding anything
recognizably truthful or useful
when this flat declarative opens before me
like a steppe and its clear, huge sky:
Boom in Headstone Business Not a Bubble.
The Department of Veterans' Affairs
electronically orders tombstones from its
three official suppliers, who must
finish and ship them within ten days. Computers
print the life-size (so to speak)

marker designs on adhesive-backed rubber sheets.
Down the line, a ten foot circular
saw blade edged with diamonds slices thirty-
five ton blocks of marble into
four inch slabs like a deli slices cheese. Then
smaller saws trim off the scrap, and
perfect uniform oblongs emerge, just as the
regulations say they should:
thirteen inches wide, three and a half feet
high, the top of each stone rounded and

smoothed by yet another machine. A worker
(yes, at this point in the process
humans enter) sticks the rubber stencil
on the stone, aligned just so, and

sends it rolling along a conveyor belt to a
booth where sand is blasted at it,
etching letters through the holes in the rubber
faster than ever chisels could,
u-shaped white grooves in white stone. The worker
sprays the letters with black paint.

All is done but polishing, boxing and shipping.
(Imagine the corpses prepared, encoffined and
shipped to where their monuments will meet them.)
Six workers do each stone,
producing ten an hour. The government's cost:
one hundred twenty dollars each.
A single supplier carves out twenty-two thousand
marble headstones every year.
There's a photo at the top of the story.
A hard-hatted worker's leaning over

a hundred twenty pallid memorial bucks.
TENZIN CHOEKU DENG KIM
floats on flawlessly metamorphosed calcite, his
branch of service and his rank, his
dates of birth and death, the decoration
PURPLE HEART he'd paid for, the theater
OPERATION IRAQI FREEDOM he'd lost his
part in. At the end, in the same
blackened sans-serif capitals as the rest:
HAIL TO THE JEWEL OF THE LOTUS.

Canto X: Statuary But Not Unmoving

I slap the paper shut, but its creased pages,
crisscrossed by crinkles, defeat my decisiveness.
Fighting annoyance and ballooning pages,
I feign patience, smoothing them with
slower, firmer hand-sweeps than are needed.
Tropical Depression Twelve
stares at me from a grey-shaded sidebar.
I look up – and stand, the paper
sliding off my lap and crumpling in the
dirt, around my feet, forgotten.

What I see is not all that dramatic.
Fifty feet away, a waist-high
gate of metal painted black, embellished with
sprays of metal elder leaves,
breaks the solemn regularity of a
fence of waist-high metal bars.
My attention's yanked beyond the fence by
rows of white stone slabs of
roughly regular size, mostly erect but,
some of them at crazed angles.

The gate opens with a bleating creak,
like a hungry cat, and slowly

swings closed as if the spring is weak that
clacks it shut behind me. Here, the
grass is raggedly cut, coarse and weedy
among the scraggly ranks of headstones
filling most of a football field's worth of space.
This isn't Arlington; no grid of
lozenges set on baize at perfect intervals,
dominoes set up never again

to fall so long as the republic stands,
unvarying in their white perfection
except in ways invisible from afar
and meaningful only to those who know
the keys to the codes inscribed upon them, those
who knew what clothed what's buried beneath.
Here are stones so old their burden of words
is lightened, shallowed, often blurred,
sometimes no longer entirely legible – beloved
son of whom we cannot say,

born in a year adrift in a decade, died either
young or old – is that an eight or a
three? – is that the round face, chubby belly and
knees of a cherub or is it a bunch of
grapes in the crowning bas-relief? – bereft of
all the official meanings incised on
military monuments; instead, the
formulas of kinship, beloved

child or parent (but always beloved), fading
into minerals uniform only by

grayness, thicker or thinner, squared across the
top or carved in scrolls or rounded.
Others, shoved over or fallen, shattered, impress the
grass with nearly geometric
chunks and shards: this one almost triangular
but for that chipped-off apex; that, a
face down parallelogram, its edges
overgrown; and this, a matriarch's,
face tipped skyward and listing her children's names but
cracked in half so one's crossed out.

Vandalism, or the work of the world? In
Plaszow, Poland, they made a pavement of
tombstones smashed into pebbles, fragments of names and
dates for the doomed to press with their feet.
Beads on a necklace, this place and Plaszow, Poland, but
I can't see the string that connects them, and
Dante's not here to tell me. A chickadee pops from
nowhere onto the tip of a stele,
cocks its head, eyes me, disappears,
zipping away in scalloped flight

over the head of an oblivious squirrel which
freezes erect at a shift in the air an
instant later, then runs, its tail caressing its

body's scalloped, bounding path,
pauses, runs, pauses, and runs some more.
Steady as ice, a small black beetle
creeps out from a blotch of leaf's shade to
stone now bright and warm with sun, then
down a green blade's curve to out of sight
among the lives that I can't see.

I remember picking tiny blueberries
off low bushes in an abandoned
graveyard going back to forest – so sweet!
There, I am certain, like here, was no-one. I
take a moment to breathe in all this absence
and the feeling of closeness to them.
A gently sinuous, gravel path entwines this
little boneyard's single axis of
symmetry like a vine on a trellis, from where I
stand to its far end. I'm at the

oblate end of either an egg or a teardrop,
depending on whether that trio of birches
and that large white object mask from here a
space prolately ellipsed or pointed.
What the hell in heaven's name is that thing?
No clues here. I go over there. The
plinth is squat, square, thigh-high concrete.
On it, a hunk of yes it's marble,
roughly pyramidal but its top is a

blob flung skywards, reminiscent

of a lava-light's glowing swimmers that sink and
simultaneously rise,
rewards my closer inspection with confusion.
Bulges and protuberances
complicate it, nowhere flat, and nowhere
bearing expressive toolmarks such as
Michelangelo or Rodin left, but a
random, variegated, heaving
surface broken by random glossy patches.
There are spots like velvet you could

brain yourself on, next to blotches jagged
as a teenager's tender emotions.
There's no sign on the plinth or elsewhere saying
what this thing's supposed to be.
Is it raw stone blasted from some quarry or
hauled from where it dropped off a cliff,
plumped down here to be seasoned by lichens and acids
delivered by rain and polluted air? Or,
was it carved by a sculptor's hand so clever
it is nowhere to be seen?

Decades ago in the city by the Arno,
I paid half a dozen visits
to the far end of a hall whose shiny
floor showed no one else's footsteps,

alone with a statue unambiguously
supremely artful. At the Uffizi,
Laocoön and his sons: do you know the story?
One of the gods was angered with him.
Why? He spoke the truth in time of war; or
maybe because he lay with a lover on

sacred grounds. He stepped out of bounds, and
so two serpents were sent to end him
where he stood, on the beach with his two boys.
The boy on the right, not yet completely
entangled, reached to slip the scaly noose
off his left ankle. It would not budge.
He turned his face to his father, pleading, trusting,
doubt rasping across his mind,
Help me! Papa, pay attention to me!
The boy on the left was swooning, held up

only by the sinuousity wrapped
around his strengthless limbs, his torso
pierced by the viper's fangs, his head lolled back, one
arm bent aloft not fallen
yet. But Laocoön looked ahead,
a gaze wrenched ninety degrees from this world,
the venom already pricking his hip, his eyes
deep pits in which his soul was drowning.
His mouth was open, but as in nightmares when one
must but cannot scream. The hallway

would have echoed with the slightest sound.
Endless slithering on his thigh and
shins, across his balls. He squirmed away from the
mouth feeding at his hip, and
pushed against that neck like flowing iron.
In the museum's filtered light a
brownish patina of dust added shading and emphasis
to the swollen-veined lumps of muscle
hopelessly straining to loosen and unloop the
oh too heavily strangling coils.

If I had known what men were not taught, to cry, I
would have. I wish I would have. I might have
made a door of this horror and beauty and might have
entered through it the world I might have
entered also through the unripened love
Victoria and I held barely ajar, or
through so many other portals winking
open my fifteenth blossoming year, from
which I shrank as if strange tongues flicked through them
(and so, had I but known, they did).

Canto XI: We're Talking Proud!

Another gate's clank behind me announces
my passage from the graveyard's gravel
paths to sidewalk pavement, summoned by a
street sign glimpsed just over the monolith's
hulking shoulder: "Cemetery Road," a
two-lane spoke on the park's green hub.
So that's the kind of sign I'm going to get.
One takes the signs one's given,
accidental correspondences or
not. Against the light, I cross the

empty road that rings the empty park.
Don't look back, I think, as if I were
leading Eurydice instead of seeking her
sister through this bleak extensive
tan and umber and brick district of duplexes.
Whimpering through the "Bush Boom," their
dogs are chained, the toys that litter porches and
yards are box store plastic, the bikes look
less expensive than their locks, the cars are
mostly dirty American beaters.

Yet, there are the grace notes, like that window

box ablaze with purple pansies, the
bathtub shrine so lovingly assembled, the
glossy orange gingerbread trim.
To my right, a blush of marigolds
conceals the cinderblock base of a signboard,
a white rectangle like a movie marquee.
Its block letters spell "WELCOME
TO ROMAN HRUSKA ELEMENTARY SCHOOL
EXEL ENCE IS NUMBER 1".

I stand at the head of a concrete walkway
connecting the sidewalk to the pillared
entrance of a sprawling, two-storied edifice.
Yellow brick. Rows of romanesque
windows. Beside the walkway, the grass is
worn away to bare dirt, as
if the traffic it carries can't be contained.
It looks like a folded up textile factory,
but for the sign. Perhaps it was. The calls of
those whose hopes include not working

there for more than another couple of years
float to me as light as lint
over the high green hedge that screens the school yard
behind a higher cyclone fence.
Trailing my fingers across its wires, I think of an
inmate rattling the bars of his cell.
The fence extends a tennis court's length beyond the

hedge's cooling shade before it
turns its corner: in that corner, on that
court, a dozen kids play dodgeball.

Half a dozen more sit on a bench
ostensibly watching and cheering their teams,
which three of them do while two of them snicker together at
nothing and one of them misses his game boy.
Two young women, chaperones, stand by talking of
something that deeply engages one; the
other's thinking of someone who's not present.
Head-size orange rubber balls
barrage the survivors on the court, who crouch and
leap and run, shrieking and laughing, to

capture projectiles that have bounced and can be
fired back, sometimes pausing
tensely to study the enemy. One boy weaves
among his team-mates a quicksilver path of
sigmoid anfractuosity, so enthralled with his
own agility he dashes
directly into an incoming ball and is benched,
his shoulder stinging where it hit.
Seated, he rehearses his vermiform routes
until his mind is full of spaghetti,

that fine comfort food, and all these losers
are far away. Meanwhile, a girl

preoccupied with hating her hair because
it's sproingy, clutches a ball to her chest,
then thrusts it, stiff-armed, into the path of the missile
streaking at her, but her shield
knocked loose caroms off her knees
across the line dividing the parties.
On the other side, a boy she'd like to
like her rushes the ball and whips it

at her, smiting her on the hip as just at
that same instant he is smitten
on the forehead and falls back bump! on his bum
surrounded by laughter. Side by side,
the couple take their places on the bench,
she in silence admiring his dash,
he loudly clowning, red-cheeked, confused.
He beat a girl: a boy beat him:
and he made everybody laugh. Compute
those ratios, if you can. Meanwhile,

the simpler world of those who still contend
grows smaller and hotter, like a
collapsing star, its glow, reflected in
the latterly ejected faces
that avidly follow its progress from the bench,
exciting their idle former team-mates
and even the chaperones into attentiveness.
Their focus feeds the remaining players'

thermodynamics. At last, one slender, swarthy
boy, intense with combative joyfulness,

faces three much bigger kids. Everyone
holds a ball; the loner stockpiles
one between his feet. They eye him and
he eyes them, as wary as cats. The
big kid in the middle and the big kid
to his left both grin and nod and
let fly simultaneously. The thin kid
fires back, stoops, and as his
ball collides with both of theirs mid-air,
scoops and whirls and flings. His last ball

bounces off the knee of the first and slaps the
calf of the second! One throw, two down! The
last of the big kids yells, "Die, terrorist!"
Her shot, already winging,
smartly whaps her foeman on his flank. The
skinny kid just stands there, stunned and
blinking like an animal just crawled out from
under a rock into the sun.
Then he tilts his head back. His eyes are focused
hard and distant, and he wears a

thin-lipped smile, a trifle bitter and private.
His shoulder blades pull back, his chest
puffs out, and slowly he raises his arms, fists clenched,

above his head, mirrored by
the three across the center line from him,
except their smiles are full-lipped, looser.
Then he lights up like a Christmas tree.
I mean, I see the strings of light
that run all through him to the star-like bundle
at the top, and brightest among them

signaling hieroglyphically, "It took three to
get me!" And the trio glows with
brilliant beacons of "Strength!" I see a shower of
photons drenching their sweaty bodies,
some absorbed, and some rebounding off their
skin or from within their eyes and
penetrating the spectators through their pupils,
setting sparks cascading on the
bench and through the laughing chaperones,
kindling within each of us who's

watching a tangled luminous synonym for
what those last combatants spell.
In my bedazzlement, I hear the taller
chaperone say, "Okay, campers,
let's go in for snacks and story time," and the
shorter, "Who's that watching at the
fence?" as if emboldened in her duty,
so I smile and yell, "Great game!" and
uncurl my fingers from the wires and shamble
inoffensively away.

Canto XII: Out of Your League

A few miles further through some developer's massively
boring enactment of the American
Dream, spottily enlivened by flares of the
residents' human amour-propre, a
yellow police ribbon and an officer
with balletic arms and a face as
blank as a demon's in hell temporarily
bar Cemetery Street,
detouring traffic down a side venue
already clogged by illegal parking.

A clot of people, lunch-hour passers-by
attracted to what they're foreclosed from joining,
watches at the tape the doings beyond. To
me they are opaque, just normal
humans of flesh and blood whose thoughts and feelings
show as ripples on a pond show
something swimming beneath, unlit. I suppose the
absence of strong emotion is why. How
odd, I think, to want an explanation
why I can't see into them: how

odd to see in them the explanation

for my lack of penetration.
Chief among the figures captivating
their attention, a young woman
drapes herself across an E-type Jaguar's
dull silver hood, leaning
back against its windshield. Her hair is like a
flock of goats descending a mountain,
thick and heavy with life and each wave
springing in place in the swaying mass.

Her eyes are blue as twin Lake Tahoes, her cheekbones
high and sharp as the peaks surrounding
Tahoe basin, her nose a proud straight ridge, her
mouth glistening red and lush as the
Rolling Stones' lips logo, her teeth as white as
kitchen appliances, her neck a
column carved in chocolate by ancient Greeks, her
shoulders bare, her skin as fine and
matte as the dashboard in the car she lies on.
Her muscular arms show she works out.

Her breasts, restrained by a band of blue
elastic fabric, loll as heavy,
firm and round as bunches of ripened grapes, her
nipples standing grape-like, proud. Her
navel, not so much a chalice as a
shot-glass, offers intoxication
sunk in a rippling, barely cushioned tummy

cradled by prominent pelvic bones. Her
groin and legs flow like dreams beneath a
tawny, sequined skirt. Now,

throwing back her head, she opens her throat to the
sky as if to receive the sun her
lover's kiss, and smiles. Her teeth are small and
clean and vivid as fresh-shorn lambs. A
short, bespectacled man approaches and orders
adjustments to the arch of her back,
displaying her fruits with different angles of thrust.
She's bored and annoyed, and if she doesn't
start getting speaking parts soon, she thinks, she might go
back to law school or maybe computers.

I hover around the fringes, avoiding body
contact that may scramble me, a
barely registered presence, nearly as
invisible as the work-shirted, dungareed
camera crew pointing their lenses at Ms. Effulgence, the
mousy-haired makeup girl, the lighting guy
fiddling with his umbrella shaped reflectors.
And all at once I see Victoria
as she stood in that Roman park, beneath the
oak, relaxed and pensive. Nearby

pulsed a guitar. Her bare feet shifted, the sound
rose through her creamy, coltish legs and

under her skirt's grey wool and the rounded yellow
cotton of her vest, emerging
with her arms aloft and graceful as flames
alive to the air, eyes closed, head tilted
in the music's dream. The birr her hips shot
through her crackled out her fingers'
snaps and ran to ground through me, a stricken
lightning rod. Flash to now, her

figure sprawled across that car beyond the
police line inert as an accident victim...
Tasting bitterness, viewing the palimpsest my
own mind scrawled upon this unknown
person's glorious body as easily as if
she were a page with barely nothing
written on it in the loosest script,
I begin to recognize my
neighbors' similar sad and layered engrossments.
Whether they measure their bodies against that

perfect prototype on the hood as if they
were themselves devices in need of
calibration; or find her falling short, as the
platinum bar that once defined the
meter lost its place to the distance a beam of
coherent light travels per one two-
hundred-ninety-nine millionth of a second
(Halle Berry's mentioned, also

Jessica Alba, in the preening tones of
connoisseurs); or size themselves on the

scales they see in their companions' eyes; or
scale their companions like fish: the thumbs of
people dead or otherwise not present
skew the balance. Tears never
were more private, but maybe he could sense them,
this young man who approaches me now,
neat in chinoes and a crisp white shirt,
bearing a smile that offers to cradle
misery like a nanny holds a newborn –
support the head! His radiance hurts,

at first. He introduces himself: street worker
for some program whose name escapes me.
Am I new to town? I am. He thought so,
something told him. I know what: my
clothes, my mismatched shoes, Salvation Army
beltless pants and untucked shirt. I
see it in his eyes. And slowly, skillfully,
never pressing too hard or relenting,
he engages me and takes my case. I
lie to him, of course. To tell the

truth (I'm newly back from hell en route to
see my dead first love, who sent for me)
might confuse him. Outlasting the thinning crowd, we

stay and talk in hope of clues. I
watch it build in him until he judges
the moment ripe and offers me
his hand. It's good to meet me. I've remembered,
Dante said you may not touch
the dead unless they let you. Thinking maybe
someone back from hell's half dead,

I try to find the place my skin stops everything
else from coming in. Instead,
there's an unclenching around the solar plexus
like a rose unfolding, and next thing
I know we are sharing manly grips,
perhaps a bit too tight. My fingers
seizing his feel subcutaneous tingles
and my eyes begin to smart.
This last could be his brightness, but that no longer
seems at odds with the rest of the day.

Canto XIII: Envy

Without Dante to hurry me, as throughout
Hell he had whenever he judged
lingering had turned to loitering,
I luxuriate in chatting
with my new friend Carlo, whose attentions
mingle professional detachment and
personal warmth in the same minty breath.
Unsure whether my rendezvous lies
fifty feet, five hundred yards, five miles, or
years away, I let him beguile me.

I assume that sooner or later he will
make me an offer I'll want to refuse, to a
shelter or clinic or feeding station, and then our
ways will part; but why he angles
with such delicate skill to keep me on the
hook while never trying to set it
escapes me, until, suddenly, all is clarified
with the arrival by his side of the
woman for whom he has been waiting
and the consequent diversion

of the greater part of his now divided
attention to her. She looks familiar, I've

known the taste of her thoughts, but it's her hair that
gives her away. Her body's concealed in a
floppy army surplus man's shirt and
loose, grey sweat pants; but here are those
rich, fat sheep, bouncing downhill.
From the paper bag she carries,
tawny fabric pokes. It's the girl on the car,
done with her shoot, rejoining her lover

who, while she was gone, improved the hour by
tarrying with derelict me.
Greeting him, "I'm ready to go now, Carlie,"
without looking directly at me, she
takes him by the elbow and pulls; but he
insists on stopping and introducing
"Sapía, light of my life." She rakes me with an
azure glance as sharp as fingernails,
then returns her smile to him, his cue to
dispose of me by offering help.

Indeed, his urge to do so has been mounting
since the moment she arrived. They
share a look, and now they're in communion
they don't mind me stepping on his
line by asking do they know if there's a
military monument near
here; my friend said I might meet him there?
Sure, they're heading that way now.

Another pause, another look. They'll take me
part way, she says. "When we part,"

he says, "you'll keep on going the way we're going –
but we won't be going that way
any more." He laughs and looks at her, and
she relaxes. "Carlie likes to
see folks get to where he thinks they should be
going, but today he promised
he'd be mine!" A flourish threads her arm through
his, and linking elbows, gaily
they march off with me a pace behind. I'm
happy here, relieved of the danger of

unexpected interpenetration,
observing their chatter, enjoying their warmth, and
watching the play of her firm, round buttocks, her muscular
thighs that stretch the surface of her
sweats and then retreat beneath the fabric, a
body unconscious of sexiness,
giving off candied wafts of the coconut grease they'd
smeared on her to save her from sunburn. I
soon might make a tent of my hospital smock, with
who knows what effect upon my

illusory trousers! Raising my eyes from this dangerous
callipygian kneading to Carlo's
and Sapía's eagerly talking heads,

soon I see what I hadn't seen when
Carlo's charms were all for me: he's obscure to the
person to whom he talks, as a man who
works a searchlight is shielded by its glare from
whomever he casts its beam upon. His
light is caught and bounced and bent and flares down the
endless, winding hall of mirrors

Sapía's personality hides within,
delighting her by the way it twinkles
in some places otherwise dark to her.
He flatters himself he sees what is hidden, but
she arranges the glasses for her own
solitary delectation, a
woman eating chocolate at her vanity.
What she loves in him most is not so
much the way he shows herself to her, but
just the same thing I see when I

look at him sideways, so to speak, undazzled:
his perfect ordinariness,
the guy in overalls who works the flood,
the one who sees right through her bosom,
if not so far as he thinks, and doesn't go crazy.
Even his lurking disbelief that a
guy like him could have a girl like this
endears him to her. A guy like him!
One in a million, acting normal around her.

I feel like someone viewing a forest

canopy from a small plane flying low, the
seemingly solidly interwoven
uppermost branches meshed and working visibly
in the breeze, the lower, heftier
limbs more loosely entwined and fitfully
disclosed, and, running to ground, the boles
that fork unseen into secretly mingling roots.
So they discuss their upcoming nuptials, with
only words and body language and memory's
lamp to read each other by.

Sapía: "So what do you think of inviting Barbara
to the reception? Barbara Anne?"
Carlo: "Isn't she the one who got that
soap – um, daytime drama – you wanted?"
Sapía: "Yeah, the millionaire's daughter who goes to
community college incognito
to learn what it's like to be a normal person.
Would have been perfect for me, right?
I was so pissed, I was so glad it flopped
before they even got around

to writing her out. She told me: they were going
to have her boyfriend rape and kill her.
She was just a part of the boyfriend's story.
Well, so now they're all at home

dreaming about their daytime emmies, and Barbara,
she was pretty broken up.
You know we went to high school together, don't you?
We were pretty tight, us two."
Carlo: "We two." Sapía, "We two, too."
She laughs and pulls him, laughing, closer.

Watching them from behind, as if from ahead
I see back to where they are, and I
want to tell them: *nobody marries for the
reasons they think they're getting married,
let alone the right ones;* and I want to
ask him: *what will be left when you find you'll
never solve the puzzle of her,* and I want to
ask her: *what will be left when his light is
just another meaningless glare;* and I want to
tear them apart and have her myself.

I want what each of them hopes will remain on that day
they can't imagine, when the whites
of her eyes are opaque as milk to him and nothing
he says can fill the space where her mirrors
hang, turning on themselves, and love's
materials are far to seek.
I envy the ignorant blundering fervor with which
they near that chrysalitic day.
Having encountered that day – for me it set the
color of all the dawns thereafter –

I envy their faith that from the first burst
of teenage sweetness through successive
disappointments jubilation builds from
error to error to this, a house
the world may safely turn in, while I sleep rough.
In sour self pity, I trudge behind them.
Is it Vicky who calls, *I'll explain?* I answer,
I want! I want! I want! I want!
Through our dead keratinous sheaths, I want
to feel how our warmths greet and mingle.

Of whom I am thinking, I am not quite sure.
All I know is that their happiness
works like an entrenching tool in the pit of my
stomach, cutting a lonely foxhole.
Into which, she lowers an elegant hand.
We've stopped at a corner. They've turned to face me.
Her grip is cool and limp, but it's enough
to pull my eyes up level with hers.
Their whites are as pure as the winter's first snow,
the irises blue you'd never drown in.

"Here is where we say goodbye," she says,
and, holding my hand, continues, "Thanks
for leaving my Carlie to me. It's funny, since
I said *I do* want to spend my life
with him, we never seem to have time together!"

Her palm has warmed to mine. Her smile
is a flood of superabundant joy. I sigh,
with what emotion I cannot tell,
and, letting slip her fingers, sincerely I wish
her all the time with her love in the world.

Canto XIV: Fathers

"You ask him." "No, you ask him." "No, you!"
"Hey man, was that Sapía Wentworth?"
No *excuse me, sir.* I look away from the
two receding backs, and scan the
approaching pair of teenage boys, one fat, one
lanky, both pimply, fourteen or fifteen, from
whom this question issued. "Who wants to know?" I
answer. The skinny one picks up the challenge.
"He does," he says, in the voice that asked. "So tell me,
why do you want to know?" I ask,

looking at him. He turns to the fat kid: "I told you!
Saw her in *Crunch Time Four,*" he says
to me, "She's the one gets pronged by the zombie.
Hottest chick ever!" he says to his friend. The
skinny kid is hyper, and if this were a
Disney movie his stolid buddy might
slow him down with well-aimed zingers, but as we
walk down Cemetery Street
together, made a group by their easy teenage
acceptance of those like me, like them

outside the privileged circles deemed fully adult –
lacking jobs, possessions, power,

dependents, sanctioned purpose, and clothes that fit – and
by the glamorous magnetism
I exert through knowing a famous hottie, the
fat kid fingers a gameboy and soon is
lost to conversation, contributes grunts at
intervals not in sync with us. The
skinny kid tells me there's no military
graveyard where I'm headed, but his

older brother knows where I can get some really
good shit, if I'm interested. I
ask him if he's sure about the graveyard.
He tells me about the time his
father took him fishing, upper reaches
of the river this town straddles,
glassy sheets of water over rocks washed
bare as teeth, teetering ankle
deep on the edge of an enigmatic pool, and
hooking tiny jeweled trout his

father enigmatically called "brownies" –
how can you call a thing so flashing
"brown" – the eloquence all in him, flashing
hidden then emblazoned in the
garish mists that cloak then open naked
on his adolescent mind. They
caught a lot of fish but brought none home.
"Catch and release," his father said, "so

there will still be fish to catch tomorrow,"
but his dad got pissy when he

said a fish would have to be pretty stupid to
let you do that to it twice.
His dad hasn't taken him since. He doesn't mind,
he says. There's one that swallowed the hook
so deep it tore out with a ripping sound.
His dad said it would be alright,
the way his dad said it would be alright
the time that mom and dad split up.
(That was unsaid.) But what about the graveyard?
Their road back home took them through pastures

grassy to the water's edge, beside the
river's winding, cat-puke green.
No point fishing here, his dad said. Trees
whose shadows sheltered scaly lives
were cut back years ago. So, no more crawling
out an overhanging limb to
dap a feathery fly, creating bulls-eyes
piscine predators couldn't ignore.
His dad said shit from towns and farms had killed
off everything below the hills.

And so – he artfully spits on the sidewalk – the kids
who dangle lines in the placid sludge
that squiggles through the city's stream-side parks

may hope to catch no more than discarded
tires and grocery carts, and deserve his contempt.
"But what about the graveyard?" I ask.
"Wait a minute," he says, "we're getting there."
"I'm not getting any younger."
This shuts him off until he decides it's a joke
and laughs extravagantly. "So,"

he says, "You gotta pay attention. Dad
and I, we crossed the Iron Bridge"
its girders' dark geometry reflected
on the river's vast smooth surface
"and stopped for lunch at the Monument. It's just this
side of the bridge. You wanna know what we
had for lunch?" He smiles *it was the last time.*
"Sure." "I don't remember. There's a
circle road that goes around the statue.
The street we're on comes off it. Me

and dad drove all the way back there to here."
"Tell me about the statue." "I
dunno. It's a statue." *Big old soldier. Horse.*
That last time his father took him, they
sat on bone-white curving slabs of marble
eating ham and cheese on white bread.
"At least your dad takes you fishing," the fat kid says,
"Mine sits on the couch and complains about ay-rabs."
A pale globular sweaty man, super

market Meat Department Manager,

loves to drink iced tea and watch the news, and
here his son stands, breathing heavily,
goaded to complaint by Skinny's ease with
exotic me, with Skinny's freedom that
he desires and hates. "Oh, fuck off, asshole.
At least your dad lives in your house,"
the skinny kid fondly replies. Yes, fondly. In each
of them a greenly glowing skein
beams at and mirrors the other. If Dante was right,
and envy is wanting what can't be shared,

then I am watching a friendship grounded in envy,
and in this City of dirty skies
and endless pavements, Dante has no words
that might untangle their conundrum.
Overhead, thunder without lightning
announces a rain of death has passed
on wings for other parts, and that is the only
voice the heavens have for us, a
voice placed there by the nimble ventriloquists who
project power in our names.

I remember that beautiful, wise man,
my father, his helplessness to more
than endure or drown emotion, his emotions
working in him like yeast on grapes.

A feeling of brotherhood sweeps me, and I chuckle
to think how the boys would recoil in horror
if they knew of my urge to hug them. Nothing
but the chuckle escapes me. It closes our
conversation like a sweet coda.
We walk together in thoughtful silence.

Canto XV: What Cannot Be Shared

The sun, a nacreous glob that floats a tad
above the rooftops, sends their shadows
stretching halfway across the street to us.
The city's a dial denoting the hour:
time for crustless cucumber sandwiches, scones
with lashings of double clotted cream
and strawberry jam, fish paste, cold salmon, cakes
and pastries, and a hot beverage
brewed from the leaves of a chinese shrub; time for
those who labor with number two pencils to

choose if (a) or (b) or (c) or nothing
is the one true answer to
push back from their desks with happy relief;
bureaucrats likewise smile, or feel the
iron bar across their shoulders tighten
beneath the weight of unmoved paper; the
first shift pops a lid or opens the door
upon a silent home or studies a
market's shelves; a mom enjoys that last five
minutes between what has been done and

what will be demanded; ditto, a dad;
the soaps give way to children's shows.

I am musing upon what can't be shared.
Dante thought the cure for grasping envy was
heavenly love, growing like compound interest to
more than match our investment in it,
distributed by the Cosmic Central Banker
to members of His holy church
as freely as Alaskan oil rebates.
That'll buy them off, he thought.

I think, *if that's what Jesus taught, two thousand
years of repeating it have not made
much of a dent.* I think of Marcus Aurelius, whose
teachings did take hold, professor of
calmly fortitudinous endurance,
and his disciple Hemingway, whose
heroes will admit the earth has moved
only after making love or
when a bomb goes off nearby, and such men
as our fathers, for whom the phrase

"I love you" was a ritual oath to be sworn on
rare and solemn special occasions.
I think of the Paradox of Thrift, how holding
back too much impoverishes
all of us. I think of the millions nightly
scanning reality tv
to glimpse a crumb of unaffected emotion,
like goldfish rising in their bowl

to gasp at the surface. I think of a circle of men
pounding hand drums around a candle,

vibrating skin and bodies of resonant wood.
Each one hits within the spaces
left by others, holding together steadily...
shifting form, direction, texture
like a flock of starlings suddenly wheeling,
zooming skyward... decrescendo...
now alighting, fingertips softly tapping, then
lightly brushing the skins, then silent,
listening now to themselves and waiting for one to
hear himself clearly enough to tell them

what he hears. "Bless this ancient circle,"
says an elder. "Bless this circle of
ancient men," quips one just turned fifty.
After the laughter subsides, he speaks of
cruel estrangement from his daughter. Shaking his
head, bewildered, he offers his pain to the
group as if placing a flower on an altar.
"Thank you, brothers," he says, and ends.
Next, a man laments his dwindling joy at
work. He was a teacher. Now, he

doesn't know just what he is, but teaching
is a lesser part each year of
what they pay him not enough to do and

don't support the doing of.
He looks forward to September no more
than the kids. This weekend, though, he
and a friend went biking, stirred the gaspingly
hot air with their passage, ate at
roadside stands beneath the dark green leaves of
summer's end, and felt there's something

more than this – he can't quite say – but it's good.
Having found that note of praise, he
rests. The savor of it prompts a man to
talk of his pride in his son, who's worked so
hard all summer landscaping, hauling rocks,
hogging brush, pruning, trimming,
mowing, digging, planting, weeding, sweating,
showering when he comes home, pulling
on a clean tee, going out with friends but
not too late. The fights they had, those

times he tried to protect them both from pains he
knew could be avoided if the
feckless little jerk would do like he told him!
Feckless little jerk no more.
Almost a man with a man's sore muscles, able to
talk with his father! What a miracle –
let go when it's time to let go, and you
find you hold them even closer.
Wordlessly, they hold him as close as they can.

Now the spirit moves in me to

share what can't be shared, to submit to this love.
It moves like a pond in which stones have dropped.
It moves like water stirred by what lives in it.
I'm going to talk about her death,
the death of my first girlfriend. I'm going to tell
how I learned she'd been cut down,
how a child can never quite believe the
words the words the words the words, and
what the price of never letting go is,
how there's nothing more than this –

"Hey, man! You alright? Hey, he's talking
to himself!" The skinny kid has
dropped behind me half a dozen paces
with his apathetic comrade.
"Hey, man! Are you tripping out, or what?"
He calls to me across this space.
"He's just a drunken bum. Let's go," the friend says.
How can I explain? I'm speechless,
plunged into silence neither calm nor loving.
They make their retreat look like indifference.

Canto XVI: The Wrathful

The boys have brought me to a roundabout.
Diametrically across,
beyond a battered traffic barrier, weeds
descend a slumping bank to a river.
Maybe half a mile away to the right, a
spidery contraption of girders carries
heavy traffic over the placid water,
vehicle silhouettes loud and tiny
against the evening. Smack in the traffic circle's
middle, an equestrian statue,

civil war vintage, I guess, from the rider's
hat, beard, cape, and sword, but
coated so thickly with what the city coughs up
what it's made of I can't tell.
To its left, men stand around a barrel.
Vivid yellow flames leap from it
and a scrawny stream of smoke that drifts
across the plaza, dissipating
before it reaches the martial rider's back
as if afraid he'll wheel and charge.

Under the dull steel sky, in this muted industrial
landscape of livid parking lots,

earth-tones and rusts and greys and featureless factory
walls behind mesh fences painted the
color the sky is now, beside this river that
upstream may as the skinny kid said
"sparkle" but here is sickened, torpid, the
tinge of mashed pigeon peas, the
barrel's crowning flames seem unnaturally
hard-edged and quick, the smoke alive.

The barrel sits in the middle of a curb cut,
blocking the entrance to a distant
building's access road that's barred already
by a wire-fence, chain-locked gate.
Twelve eyes quietly watch me approach, and no one
utters a greeting. Some of them shift to a
man whose back is to me. He turns, huge,
round-faced, with pock-marked cheeks, cleft chin, and a
nose as broad and flat as a shovel, that looks as
though a collision with heavy equipment

formed it – much to the worse of the heavy equipment.
"Joe Hill," he says. He's seventy, maybe,
silver-haired, gentle-voiced, cleanly
clad in denim overalls the
same, I guess, that he wears every day, like
some might wear a business suit
although retired because it's what they do.
He offers a hand I could put both mine in,

skin the hue of bog iron, walnut shell knuckles.
I feign a cough and wipe my palm

on my illusory pants leg. "Got a cold,"
I say. "Don't want to give it to you."
"That's right thoughtful. Did you bring a potato?"
I can tell how blank I look from
how he laughs. My intermittent gift of
reading others extends to emotions,
not to random queries about vegetables,
although... although, there's something here.
"I didn't think that you was one of us.
Hell, I know everybody was

a brother Local Seventy Five, and you're
not one," he says. I say, "No, I'm
just passing through here on my way to heaven."
"Ain't we all." "Well... now you've got me
wondering, why you brothers would be spending a
fine late August evening like this
hanging outside the gate of a shuttered factory
baking potatoes in a barrel?
I call you brothers, although I've never held
a union card. My grandpa gave

his life to the I.L.G.W.U.
He'd say, you kids don't know the struggle.
Now I'm old enough to wish I'd known

enough to listen to his memories,
take them in, and make them part of my life; but
that kind of wisdom doesn't come
until you're filled with things you can't forget
and fear that they could be forgotten.
What will be left? You might get mad at the little
bastards who won't give you their time."

"You got that right. Damn kids!" He chuckles, thinking.
"I don't know why you'd care about this,
stranger, but you hit the nail why I would
want to tell you. So I will.
After I got back from my tour in Korea –
speaking of things a man would rather let
go and be gone – I didn't ask to go and
nobody gave much of a damn when
I returned, except my folks, of course –
I got a place at this here mill

and every working day for fifteen years
the Number Five bus set me down
right here, Gate Thirteen B. The sign's on the wall
at Casey's Bar, now. I'd walk up
this drive to the changing room and prepare for my shift.
Now you say 'brothers', let me tell you
as a black man not a lot of brothers
on the floor or in the union,
but I made it because the Local's Treasurer's

son and I was overseas

together. We seen some things, you know what I mean?
He said he could take care of me
when we got home. I didn't think he would,
but he did. So I owed my job and my union
card to a white man. How else would I get them?
Mostly I'll say it wasn't too bad.
Nobody messed with my man Dan, so mostly
nobody messed with me. Mostly
nobody had too much to do with me,
at all. Like Jackie Robinson,

I kept my head down, did my job as good
as I could do it, never, never
let them pathetic cracker bastards rile me
to where they could see it. Bought myself
a damn fine case of hypertension! Paid
a mortgage, kept my wife at home,
raised my kids – three boys and a girl – to never
miss a meal or lack for clothes, and
they've got professional jobs and she is married."
He almost says, *I don't regret*

the loneliness, to look at them, but can't,
and pauses, wondering, *Is it true?*
Only when I look at them, he decides.
"Along about nineteen sixty-nine,

things got ugly, same as they always do when
management starts to feeling heat and
comes to the shop floor with that look in their eye.
The why of it don't bear going into.
Work rules tightened, break times policed, bust
your ass is what is expected, contract

talks begin and all they say is giveback,
tension up and down the line,
bust a sprocket it might mean your job,
ease it off they chew you out.
Ain't nobody singing mornings in the
changing room. It's bad quiet...
I kept on keeping my head down and my eyes
wide open, but something was going to blow,
and when things blows, it always lands on the nigger."
"We say, no matter what happens, they always

blame the Jews." "Is that so? Depends
on who's the handiest target, I guess."
A black-and-white newspaper photograph from the sixties,
bearded Abraham Joshua Heschel, his
froth of white hair crammed beneath a beret,
standing alongside the baby-faced, neatly
moustached, sad-eyed Martin Luther King,
flickers behind my optic nerves.
I wonder if it flickers behind his.
His shoulders relax. He leans forward.

"The nigger talk started up again before
the strike. I'd almost got to think
they didn't even notice any more,
but now the grab-ass horsing around
would stop as soon as I got close, and eyes
would slide away from me and down,
you know what I mean, and conversations fade,
and the couple of guys who treated me normal
stood way out and backed off some. Only
Dan was same as ever, mostly.

That got better when we went out and I
stood with them. That was a rainy April.
Mornings, Dan and I would share a thermos
on the line – I still remember
how the steam would rise around his fingers,
unscrewing the top – hot and strong.
But when the company got the court to call
us wildcat, well... everybody
got real quiet, watching to see what I'd do.
They'd gave us fourteen days to give

in, come back, save our jobs... or else.
You know what I mean. Each man on that
picket line was thinking it over, and each man
on that line made out as if
he had doubts about no one but me.

Even Dan, except with him, he'd
make like it's a joke. That cuts real bad,
to think about it now, but then,
I thought, *I always knew that boy's a honky,*
angry, crouching into myself

like Ali when he's doing the rope-a-dope.
Every morning, we still shared that
coffee. It cost him, sharing that coffee with me.
I knew just what it got him a taste of, and
I was glad of it, and grateful, too.
Bitter times. So, back on the line:
it was a Thursday evening, we show up here,
at this here gate, a kind of ambush,
unexpected like, to catch the shift change,
see if we can stop the scabs.

Cool and drizzly, the air's all dull with water and
everything's glossy and wet and the pavement's
greasy slick, you know what I mean? Your windshield
wipers just smear it around, the lights are
all too bright and blurred, and after fifteen
minutes on the line your clothes is
damp right through and the sign you're carrying flops
right off its pole, the cardboard's soaked
and the staples kind of melt right through it.
Then is when the scabs show up,

two or three to a pickup, driving slow and
steady through the line and into the
gate where we can't follow them and then they
gun it. The boys get madder and madder,
watching those tail lights disappear up that drive.
So, here comes a brand new, two tone
F-100, just one face in the cab, and
somebody couldn't stand it no more.
Throws a brick. The cops haven't got there, yet.
The windshield crazes, you can't see nothing

behind it, the F-100 swerves and next
you know its bumper's pinning Dan
to the fence right over there and he's as white
as a gutshot corporal I saw at Hungnam.
The truck rolls back a bit, and Dan is yelling
he's alright, but he's grabbed onto
the fence, just hanging there, and next I know
I've tore the cab door open, I've grabbed
the driver's shirt and hauled him out. He's limp
as a sack of potatoes, I'm holding him up.

I look around behind me. All these strange,
white faces, wild with fury.
I felt I could do anything to that kid.
He's maybe twenty, blue-eyed, curly
black hair like a Spanish movie star,
can't move his mouth he's scared so shitless,

just keeps going *uh... uh... uh...*
So, I set him to his feet.
I brush the glass off of his shoulders. I say,
'Now, son, you'd best be going home.'

The boys all part to let him pass, and he walks
like his knees don't work so good.
Sometimes I wonder what ever happened to him.
Me, that moment I held him there
I stopped being mad with anybody ever
except those greedy motherfuckers
sets us working people against each other.
A couple years later, they busted the union.
The year after that they closed the plant, so a hell
of a lot of good it did them, and every

year since then us wildcats that are left, we
meet on this spot, where Dan got his ruptured
spleen he died from that summer." He's glaring at me,
breathing hard. I wait for him to
come to himself. I say, "Brother... forgiveness..."
and stop, confounded. "Oh, I'll forgive
the suits alright," he says, and a grin splits his lower
jaw from his upper, "I'll forgive the
suits the day they ask me nice," and claps me
on the shoulder and hands me a spud.

Canto XVII: Smoke and Morals

I saw it coming and steeled myself and so
I feel my shoulder fraternally warmed
and little more, although perhaps I steeled
myself too much, as he withdraws
his hand abruptly and gives me a curious look.
But now the beers come out of the cooler.
The rest of the evening's given over to
hilarity and nostalgia, including
a lengthy, circumstantial discourse on why
our feast this night is baked earth apples.

I manage to conceal my lack of consumption.
At length they repair to a bar to complete
anesthetizing the fractures, wounds and abrasions
intimacy might have healed
if men were taught to embrace their humanity
instead of trained to overcome it.
After I have declined a second time Joe's
invitation to "really join the
brotherhood" at what "now we're retired
we do best," Joe starts to swing his

hand for a parting shoulder slap – the nearest
he can manage to a manly
hug – but hesitates halfway and flops it
to his belly, which he scratches.
"'Bye, then," he laughs. And then I'm alone with the statue.

Not quite. The gloaming has deepened to dusk
    in this abandoned sector so sparsely served
  by the streetlamps that elsewhere obliterated
    with their ignition all of evening's subtly
      deepening gradations. A few stars prick

the city's bubble of photon pollution. Around
    the statue, evenly spaced, ten forms
of roughly human size and shape glow feebly,
    tints on the air, radium green,
as still as sentinels. Angels? If so, how dim,
  how diminished from the unbearable
brightness that ushered Dante up his mountain,
    from the beings of lethal greatness
  known more recently to Rilke. Auras
    departed from the bodies they guarded?

Their animation seems permanently suspended.
    Aware? Of what? And to what end?
  Nothing gives them meaning, yet they have it.
    As I circle their circle, pondering
whether and how to test their inscrutability,
    from the dark between the horse's
  forelegs, a narrow, almost gothic arch, a
    voice calls, "*Vieni. Ci si aspetta.*"
Ducking low, I enter, and once I've writhed
    between the knobby knees, I hear

a space that echoes hugely. Straightening up,
I clunk my head quite hard, and when
my eyes will open they do not see. "*Vieni*,"
Dante's gentle voice repeats,
"and in the morning you'll regain the means
of knowing whether too much light
is what impairs your vision, or maybe too little.
For now, that faculty rests. Enjoy
this time we have between, and talk with me.
Tell me how it is to walk through

places that once were buried, the roots of the beautiful
mountain that grew where the earth fled Satan.
The pains of climbing it were only the pains
of leaving behind what kept us from heaven.
Some of us, loved, were feeble to love in return.
Some of us, loving the fruits of love,
were distracted from love itself. Some of us
loved wrongly. Each, at climbing's end,
forgot and was forgiven. The mountain's gone.
What do you find, on your flat streets?"

"Mountains of faith erode much faster than those
pushed up by plate tectonics," I say.
"The mountain formed by Satan's falling through
the core of the earth might better be likened
to an igneous intrusion than an
upthrust plate," comes his rejoinder,

"but, you're right, yet it erodes.
I note that your voice has found its feet.
And now that a day of eternity stands between
my time and yours, and little birds

fly above this plain of rubble where rose a
mighty rock, I ask again,
my son, how fare the souls who pass through here?"
*Tell us yourself, Mister Sub
Specie Aeternitatis*, my grandfather's voice
rumbles from somewhere, but something in my
master's tone subverts one-upmanship. He
cares to find out what I think.
"Those whom you found doing hard time
circumambulating your

Mount Purgatory's penitential ledges
knew why they were there and what they
suffered for. Anger? Sure – and after a
couple hundred years of shuffling
on that shelf through bitter smoke and moral
exemplars they'd be ready to take
a step towards heaven. Do you remember the proof
you offered of your religion's truth?
Rome turned Christian, and with it the world,
suddenly as a tulip opens!

Well, we now know things were not so simple.

I mention this not to change your mind,
which, I know, is beyond changing – " "True,
but only in a limited sense."
" – but to suggest that some of your assumptions
that seemed to you as solid as rock
may have been as contingent as flower petals."
"I see that now." "Of course you do.
And so many petals have fallen! Meadows, fields,
pastures brilliant with all the wild

flowers human thought can conceive! But autumn
comes to every one, and winter.
Blue and white, yellow, red, and orange,
wilts, turns brown and hard, and crumbles, and
composts next spring's spectacle. You saw mankind as
numberless points on a single continuum,
graded by weight, color and type on a scale from
Satan to God, as if those two were
clasps at the ends of a string of beads that stretched past
all horizons of space and time.

Now the clasps are lost; the string is broken; the
beads are scattered all over the globe,
black and white, yellow, red and brown. I
look at them and see the shreds of
string you tried to tie them with, weaving
serpentine, graceful, useless loops.
What could ever bind them in a pattern? As

soon as a pattern emerges, it changes. In
motion unceasing, their color, size and shape
shift with the light, their neighbors' shadows, their

own internal workings; and then they fade, but
never quite to nothing; and everywhere
new ones pop up, but never from nowhere.
And look again: numberless filaments
run through each to each and all the others: a
beadwork shawl and not your single
recursive strand. And look again: the fibers
stretch or thicken, fray and heal or
snap! And again: your 'beads' are rather knots the
web has tangled on itself."

Canto XVIII: Loose Ends

Unsure if I have answered his question, I pause.
"By placing Lucifer on a par
with his Creator," says my guide, "as equal
extremes, your metaphor implies
the Albigensian heresy, but knowing
you reject that false doctrine
together with the true one, I let it pass."
"If I were Catholic, I'd be Pelagian,"
I say with a smile. "And banished for it, too,"
he answers, with an emotion obscure

to me, "but can you not conceive of one
great unifying twining
of all these little interconnecting strings
that you hypothesize, that I
might recognize as God?" "Well, that would be
your superstring theory, wouldn't it?
And no more provable than the one in physics."
"You privilege knowledge over faith.
But something about your doctrine bothers me,
more than your mere agnosticism.

Doubt is kin to wisdom, after all.
But where, in all your web of relationships

pulling hither and yon, is freedom of will?
In those lint balls cast from and clinging
to the fabric of being, to which you would
reduce us, where is room for a soul?"
"I had a friend, a woman of perfect faith.
You would have liked her. A thousand years
after the Great Schism, she still splutters
indignantly at 'the power-mad pope.'

So beautiful, so passionate, so Greek!
It pained her that I could not find
a way to love her Jesus as she did.
It pained me, too. We stood across
a chasm from each other, which she had leaped.
If she could have reached a hand to
me and pulled me over, she would have done it,
and if my fingers could have grasped
instead of lightly brushing the tips of hers,
we might have swung me over there.

Instead, our arms extended, I waved good-bye
to all the joy she promised and
her incommunicable experience of faith,
which might be shared but only with those
who already have it. May she find such a mate.
I would no more doubt her feelings'
truth, that Christ is god, than I can believe it."
"If her eyes did not reflect the

light of heaven into yours, bless that
painful moment you stayed on your path."

"Which brings us to the question of free will.
Philosophers kick it around, these days,
deny that it exists. They argue our choices
are made for us by forces within us
we do not control and barely acknowledge.
Sure - at least a hundred must have
yammered contentiously in me for several months
before that 'farewell' crossed my teeth,
from being born to a stiff-necked people, to
my grandfathers' stern rejection not only

of moshiach but also Israel's Yahweh,
to my hunger for a life not
desiccated by lack of spirituality,
to the loves I formerly had and
how she seemed both like and unlike any,
to the flavors of our pleasures,
to the little bump on the back of her neck when she
bows it and the downy hair that
covers it like the golden summer grass on the
gentle hills of Napa County.

Perhaps an algorithm might account
for all those forces' valences, strengths,
and vectors; perhaps a computer could run it

and say what my decision was.
Will it have done the same thing I did? Why
have millions of years of evolution
given me this sense of weighing teetering
outcomes, if they're predetermined?
Impotent sentience wouldn't enhance one's prospects
for survival or reproduction.

It would be a lifelong prisoner gazing
out a window too high to reach at
uncontrollable chaos – miserable, helpless,
passive, useless to itself,
unable even to die of its own accord.
Its highest hope might be to achieve
detachment indistinguishable from insanity.
Not for it, our life of muddling with
more or less pleasure among confusing choices.
Some would argue that we who cannot

claim to have made ourselves the selves we are,
consequently cannot claim the
credit for acting according to our wont. Their
callow cleverness no more persuades me than
Zeno's 'proof' that motion gets you nowhere.
There's a difference between what happens
when the doctor hits me on the knee
with his little rubber hammer, and
when I kick a philosopher in the ass."

"You seem to have some feelings about this."

"Yes. I want to say, misuse of intellect
irks me, but that's not completely honest.
Anger's mostly indifferent to intellect's uses.
I hate the suggestion that all this pain is
no more than the friction a pawn feels
grinding from one square to another, that
all our careful moral accountancy merely
papers over an absent principal,
that my intricate story of causes and reasons is
missing a narrator: ego, scared of

being taken out of the picture, being
silent, inert, dispersed, dead."
I pause, and notice the absence of traffic noises.
Perhaps the hour is very late.
A certain expectant quality fills the silence.
"You asked me about another thing, too.
I must confess, of this I'm not so sure."
"Of course not. You hesitate even to name it."
"The word seems to lose its breath before it climbs
the back of my throat. But if we're talking

about Aretha Franklin, Otis Redding,
the reverend Solomon Burke, the joyous
Little Richard, and what poured from their hearts
and shook this uptight white boy down

to the wondering roots of my... well, my soul... it leaps
athletically forth," I finish lamely.
He leans in. "Are we not talking about those singers?"
"But it seems too easy and slight: a
feeling no one could describe or locate,
emerging from somewhere beneath the notes,

between the tones, behind the beat of tunes
written mainly to be sold.
Set *that* in the scales against the science they teach
in school, and you will need eleven
thumbs to make the balance come out even. "
"Your neuroscientific authorities
teach that self awareness flows from processes
biochemically bioelectric or
perhaps computational in nature
(they're not sure which) within your brain,

no way dependent upon a hidden mystic
observer and manipulator
pulling the strings of self from behind the scenes.
They locate soul in the gaps that are left by
incomplete mechanistic explanations.
They would do better to look beyond
the precincts of their theories. There resides
a class of mental events that they
denominate 'qualia' – feelings in all senses
of the word: the depth of purple; the

thrill of vermillion; the hot, damp, spicy
sweetness of breathing summer's air in
Toscana; crescendo and decrescendo of
human experience; light and heavy
hearted, headed, handed; the blues, as you call it;
dimensionless, ephemeral, and
therefor beyond the grasp of any instrument
science can muster, but no less real for
dancing free of empiricism's grapples.
That is where to look, if truly

they're looking for soul." I'm getting sleepy. I murmur,
"Sometimes, when I'm sitting, breathing...
air moves like a tide, back and forth
through my nostrils... I have been watching
streams of thought pass likewise, like clouds, I mean...
without my conscious intervention...
I descend through layers of cloud... I land in a
place beneath the clouds, of clarity.
Nothing obscures my vision of what is there: a
living room; a cat that silently,

motionlessly stalks a dust mote; squares of
sunlight sliding across the floor; a
man who sits cross-legged on a bench and
other times is me, but now,
between all thoughts and feelings, is not me, is

simply aware of... well, aware.
Touchdowns like that last a second – less –
before the mental bungee yanks and
there I am again...." Like stones on strings,
my words pull me down towards sleep.

Riding through layer after darkening layer, I
hear my docent whisper, "You ask
if our human essence is your soul, or
if your soul is what is left when
what is human has all slipped away.
What you ask is beautiful and
proper and a mystery that exceeds my
present ability to answer.
Victoria may be able to help with this.
When you find her again, remember."

Canto XIX: The Avaricious, Part One

I am spread-eagled in the air, high
above earth's mottled blue and green.
Perhaps a high-flying aircraft has shoved me out,
so high I seem to float not fall.
The air which should be screaming past my ears
whistles soft as distant flutes.
At my back is something so deep it scares me.
Before me hangs that moldy thing.
I weave and spin like a milkweed seed on the breath
of the Anemoi singing me their names:

*Nothing is here for sure. Nothing for sure is
here. Nothing here is for sure.
Nothing is for sure here.* Something
slips by so fast
it's gone before I can grab it. The air's as full of
beings as Dorothy's Kansas twister,
possible bodies and faces of smoke and their lives
whooshing past too quick to know.
How will I ever remember to tell you about it?
Winds as wild as bumper cars

carry houses but stepping through the front door
every time I step through the front door

the gods and knowledge living there are different
and must explain again. I walk the
hall to the empty room at the rear of the building
and peek out the little high window
to find out who's that yelling, and through it shines
the far earth's mottled blue and green,
and mid-calf up Italy's fancy ruffled boot
Dante yells it's solid where he is.

Dante yells, "It's solid!" Where he is,
Dante yells. It's solid, where he is
Dante. I open my eyes to the morning's light, and
everything behind them dissolves, so
I am startled to see that angular visage
leaning over me, in one piece, and
unsurprised when it disappears in stages like
Alice's Cheshire Cat, leaving at
last two lips as thin as mating snakes that
say, "Across the bridge and ahead."

I roll from under the horse's belly into its
shadow, and stand. No traffic here, but the
bridge bristles with boxy silhouettes
creeping, and lowing like distant cattle.
Although I'm eager to go, I hesitate
for one last view, panning the former
factories' walls, their high up broken windows that
let in birds and rain, the weed-fringed

gaps between their bulks, the fences topped with
tinsely coils of razor wire

ringing expanses of empty, cracked pavement
around the empty, industrial carcasses
to protect their owners' shares of emptiness.
Nothing golden's to be found here.
Mayn rue platz – I hum a bar, and leave,
but the song's sad Yiddish lilt
stays with me – *vu lebns velkn bay mashinen
dortn iz mayn rue platz...*
I walk a little slower than the river
flows, bemused by sweatshop ghosts and

puzzling at my last night's dream as a plastic
jug and a beer can glide on by.
Froth draws pale lines on the murky waters.
I'm thinking how hard we cling to nothing
that can be held, for fear of letting go
and fear of what will then be found
when nothing solidifies around us like amber,
and thinking how I hate the rich.
I hate their insistence that their desire to have
more than anyone else may need must

supersede another's hunger, illness,
raggedness, misery, ignorance, cold. Their
servants shovel the filth of their leavings into

everyone else's yard; and we are
all their servants; and it's piled the deepest
where the lowest among us live.
I hate the way we scramble to be like them.
I hate their pride. I hate their cruelty.
How they stand on other people's shoulders
and take credit for being farsighted!

They make government their bitch and plaything,
and claim it's for the common good.
They keep to themselves what the poor most need, and when
from lacking the means to soften their lives
the poor are toughened, stunted, and deformed
they damn the poor for being so damaged.
I hate their hypocrisy and I hate their charity,
giving to whom they deem deserves it
what they deem will make them go away
in quiet and leave their wealth undisturbed.

I have known some children of the rich
who had not accepted their riches.
There was the boy who pickled his brains in acid
and gave away his money to
professionals in the business of doing well
by telling the rich how best to do good.
There was the boy who loaded his pickup truck with
lobsters to share with those who let him
think they were his friends. There was the girl who

gave herself to drink and poems.

Each a perfectly normal, fucked-up kid.
Never could I have hated them, but
I could dedicate my life to their
destruction as a class. "Class:" an
alien concept, here in the self-styled land of the
self-made, of law's majestic equality.
But it's a given my grandfathers brought with them
from Europe's bloodlands, and like the immigrants
run ashore at Plymouth Rock, whose sour
theism New England's winters seemed to

plainly ratify, my granddads saw no
reason to abandon the plank on
which they'd floated to Ellis Island, Houston, and
thence to Manhattan, Chicago, and other
places palpably inegalitarian.
I would like to see the rich
brought to a world where nothing owns them, standing
on a jetty, holding perhaps an
unfamiliar fruit a vendor has sold them,
lost, confounded by possibility.

My reverie collapses at the foot
of the bridge's portal's left-hand I-beam.
The rust-scabbed girder leans away to bear its
pot-holed deck across the river.

Uprights are missing from the pedestrian railing.
Clearly, this city's fathers' faith is
firm that the people's money's better spent on
cell phones and video games than taxed to
maintain what everyone uses and nobody owns.
Where the sidewalk's concrete ends, a

metal walkway begins. Against its oxidized
rouge grate, the river, green as
wilted cabbage, looks like long-past Christmas.
I am fascinated briefly.
Here's a fluid quietus I might plunge to,
with the aging bridge's members.
That won't do. I look ahead. Beside me,
four lanes: the near two empty; the
far side a shiny stream of stalled impatience
encased in steel en route to shop.

Canto XX: The Avaricious Get Another Part

I lean against another rusty I-beam.
Behind me, the weary span. Spreading
before and below me, acres of commerce. Cars
dribble off the bridge, received by
multiple thoroughfares converging on it.
An over-eager SUV
nearly swipes me with its side-view mirror,
turning sharply to one of many
twisty little one way lanes down there, a
confusion of alleys tangled as

the root-ball of a fallen, ancient pine.
The only way ahead is through.
I follow. A moustached Kazakh calls to me,
half-hidden by his mounds of walnuts,
cashews, peanuts, hazlenuts, chestnuts, pecans,
brown and tan beneath the red and
white striped awning of his four-wheeled cart.
Next to him, a Tibetan woman's
blanket on the pavement's spread with gaudy,
ceremonial swords and daggers,

beadwork trinkets, and half a dozen Michael
Jackson CDs in cracked jewel cases.

Better to cross the street if you're after music.
There, the brilliantly draped Somali
woman's filled a stack of plastic milk crates
with LPs, CDs, cassettes and
eight tracks, DVDs, and paper-sleeved 45
r.p.m. singles. Her yellow, blue and
orange guntiino matches one of the vibrant
bolts a Sikh has piled on sawhorse

tables under a tent nearby, the other
side of the booth where the toothless Chinese
man is frying little wooden skewers of
marinated squid on a griddle and
scenting the street with five spice powder,
charcoal smoke, and hot oil.
People step around a fat black man who
squats behind a didgeridoo
teasing from the circle of his breathing
intricate geometries that

buzz into the air and through our bodies; a
cardboard shoebox by his side
contains a sparse collection of varied coins.
By him, a Florentine dealer in leather
wallets, gloves and purses dances, skip-step,
juggling customers, haggling three ways
all at once and calling to passers-by
over the pitter-patter of chatter.

Acres and acres of it. A woman pounces
on a bargain and crows to her friend. A

man complains to the world at large as god's his
witness (hoping the women will see and
if they see will admire his performance) his bag of
pistachios isn't full enough.
Two teenage girls in tank tops giggle
over a really cute bustier.
Three teenage boys lark by, hunting
digital mayhem and eyeing sidelong the
girls' flabby midriffs. The girls fall silent,
abruptly engaged with piles of sweaters.

The boys grow louder. One of them flips a cigarette
butt between the feet of a man with
distant eyes who stands in the middle of the
street repeating "Change? Spare change?"
To him, the boys are vacant air. He picks out
shabby me among the approaching
throng but, seeing no competition, relaxes.
I walk past without eye contact.
Not a hundred feet beyond him, I stop.
I'm lost. I don't know where I am.

Ahead is through is fine when you're outside it,
hundreds of acres of narrow, wriggling
streets crawling with people seeking their wants,

interacting without connecting.
I have no desire this place can meet.
Where is Victoria? Where is Dante,
harsh with pain and soft with love, and wise?
I'm standing crying in the street.
People are giving me distance the way they do
to avoid the hungry spare change man,

the black hole at the center of this galaxy.
*Maybe we won't be sucked in, if
we don't look at him.* They fool themselves.
In their slowly decaying orbits,
whether or not their eyes are drawn to his,
they are ruled by what rules him.
The hot, tight tears of frustration give way to
compassion's gentler, stronger flow.
Then, drained of hope and purpose, I look around.
A Peruvian wearing a broad, flat hat

has set out on the sidewalk rows of plastic
jugs that hold a yellow liquid,
gasoline, beside a stack of half a
dozen gleaming steel camshafts.
A cluster of men and boys inspects them critically.
Just beyond, I see a cartload of
pineapples, and, on top of the mound, a head.
A female head with big blonde hair
rests among the fruits and their stiff green leaves, its

blue eyes open and slightly downcast.

The head begins to levitate. I think,
This is it, the final crumble;
meaning deserts me in appetite's agora.
I brace my mind for worse outrages.
Instead, a pair of navy blue clad shoulders
and a graceful, slender neck
trail the head upwards; a sensible shopper
rising from scrutinizing fruits as
if to retort, *yes, but in meaning's absence,*
judgment waxes most fastidious.

Why not let a head lead me ahead,
I think, and hurry after my power-
suited bellwether. Swiftly she strides through the
jumbled jungle of buyers and sellers.
Done with the small-time hawkers, she puts them behind her.
Leaving their district, she crosses a plaza
without sparing a glance for the pair of enormous
copper ellipses like a giant's
ear rings that stand upright at its center,
placed by some corporate Ozymandias.

Immense, simple forms of marble, granite,
and tinted glass surround us, bearing
discrete small signs announcing establishments
whose names will tell you nothing unless

you know already what they are and then
they say, congratulations, you're here!
She pushes through a smoky, glossy door.
Within, it's very clean and quiet.
The carpet she stands on, looking left and right
as if the persons expected to welcome

her by name were unaccountably late, is
deep underfoot and several shades deeper
than her suit; display cases (of glass so
clear its existence must be inferred)
seem to float on it. Gleaming metal frames
outline oblongs through which she views,
arrayed on blackest velvet, expensive sparkles,
sharp in the room's hushed lighting. And
yes! it calls to her by name, the ghost that
hovers just above a brooch –

porcelain rosebud set amidst diamond sprays –
so like the one her mother promised
her older sister the nurse aide never could
be proven to have stolen, it hurts
to look at, but sweetly, because her sister never
got it and now the decision who will
have it will be hers. The clerk politely
hands her back her card, rejected.
The clerk, brown eyes downcast, apologizes
when it fails a second time.

The clerk agrees to try a second card.
The clerk agrees to try a third.
It fails. The room grows dim, except this spot
as bright as crystal. She cannot think
what can have happened. She hears the clerk agree,
and hears the faintest curl of amusement,
as if it were the tip of a bullwhip unfurling
past her cheek. She spins away and
spies me looking in the window, and shivers,
feeling naked and alone.

Canto XXI: Statius

Fearful of being marked for a stalker, I straighten
slowly, facing away from the window, and
walk away upstreet to a shabby kiosk where
cleaners, clerks, and others who serve the
people who think of this district as theirs can wait for
buses in shelter from rain and sun.
This time of day, I have the bench to myself.
I lean against the plushy lips
a poster would have me believe belong to a woman
who's found the right toothpaste. I'm as empty

as the shirtless young man on the opposite
wall is full of purported mirth
at the sight of a can of his favorite beer.
Of which, one's crumpled beneath the bench.
I contemplate what kind of happiness
ensued in its flattening, and when
I've sucked that contemplation dry, I notice
something's joined me on the bench.
When I describe it as a smudge, I am
afraid, dear reader, you will imagine

those tangled demons, like man-sized steel wool scrubbers,
we encountered throughout Hell.

This is something else. The size of the thing keeps
changing, though mostly it flutters around a
sort of a core the rough dimensions of a
medium human adult male.
It's like a squall of confetti, or diamond-dust snow.
After a while, I decide it's sitting.
At that moment, the woman exits the store, her
cheeks a pink her navy blue

suit sets off well. Heading our way, her
eyes catch mine for the splittest of seconds.
Then, she hurries past, attention absorbed in the
transfer to her shoulder bag of a
small, black gift-wrapped box. The spectre
beside me, unseen by her, leans to me, and
asks, in a clear, soft drawl, "Friend of yours?"
"I wouldn't have thought so five minutes ago,"
I answer. I wait. It volunteers nothing. I ask,
"Do I... did we... are we acquainted?"

"I don't recall we ever met, when meeting
meant a little more to me
than it does now I'm somewhat more... we'll say,
diffuse. It takes some getting used to, this
spreading out. If that's what you want to call it.
Sorry. I've lost the knack of being
seen and talking, since my untimely demise.
I should have said, my name was Statius

Sneath, and I was a scribbler. Greeting cards,
    some freelance travel pieces, jingles,

catalogue copy. You've surely seen my work.
    And late at night, of course, the poems
I thought would keep my soul alive, that saved
    this part from burning with the ads.
You're not likely to have encountered them,
although my friends posthumously published
a small collection that spread my small renown
    to the parish borders, and beyond.
Happy to be here, friend. And you? I hope
    that you don't mind if I remark

how rarely someone in your state of health,
    that is, so far from death's door, pokes
    his toe across the sill enough to say
    a hearty hello to the likes of me."
So, I relate my story: how, while drifting
    from fecklessness to inanition,
I blundered into despair; where, I was found
by a messenger sent by her through whom
love sang to me its first, most piercing notes;
    and how, recalling her to me,

he set about recalling me to her;
our slog through the loveless wastes they make
who looking at the world see only mirrors;

        my crazy hope my skin again
    may trace her long lost, vibrant, lovely sweetness;
   but since we arrived in this muddled city,
his guidance, which through hell was clear and constant,
     has turned vague and fleeting; how strangely
      altered I am since we fled the netherworld
        into this middle earth; I say,

    "Falling out of the pit, I felt scraped thin.
      The hope of seeing her was all
   that held me up inside. But now, I'm lost.
  I feel I'm swimming through muddy waters."
  Statius' response is to sing a few bars of blues:
    "I'll drink muddy water, sleep in a hollow
    log... drink muddy water, sleep in a hollow
    log... I'll be your man, babe, sure won't
  be your dog... and might I ask what you call
      this afterlife chaperone or docent

  or cicerone? Should I call him your Virgil?"
   "You're almost right," I say, and I name
the astounding company I've been keeping. If
    you can imagine a cloud of multi-
colored motes gasping and clapping, that's Statius.
    Yes, he's a fan. We pass a delicious
hour feeding each other the grapes of our mutual
      admiration for the Master,
during which time a few people enter the kiosk and

quickly decide to wait outside

rather than share the space with the crazy man
talking poetry to himself,
except one high school kid who hunkers in
the farthest corner and quietly listens
to my side of the conversation. Statius:
"I will stick to you as close as a
fly on shit, if it means I'll meet that man!"
I laugh; and, since it's been so long,
and since it feels so good, I let it roll.
Just as a river in spring flood

will bear away on its brawny, brown back
whatever littered its frozen winter
along with all it tears from its slumping banks,
everything from twigs to trees,
it carries a lot of emotional debris.
Between its waves, I gasp, "You catch
a lot more flies with ho... ho... honey!"
What the kid is making of this,
I'd know if I cared. "I did not mean to imply,
that is, I do apologize if,"

Statius says, which starts me off again.
I reach to hug him around the shoulders,
but at my sudden movement the teenager flinches,
and I think better of trying to clap

a blizzard on the back. My arm falls, limp,
and with it my spirits. "You'll have to wait
at least 'til dark. The daylight drowns him out.
And maybe I'm nowhere near the right place.
All he told me was go ahead."
"Ain't been walking backwards, have you?

What you're saying is, he promised if you
keep on trying to get closer
to where he means to bring you, you'll see him again."
"Aaah!" I hadn't thought of that.
The kid is wondering what has wrung this long-drawn,
surprised ejaculation from me.
Am I in pain? He's scared to ask, and scared of
my increasing displays of emotion.
I sit and watch Statius silently scintillate. Maybe
his scintillae can lead me ahead.

"Some people get a pillar of fire, a column of
smoke," I say, "but I get you."
He laughs. "George Bailey did alright with Clarence."
We talk. He says that hell has left me
"one foot in and one foot out the grave" and
"that's the reason others' inner
bitterness and sweetness hit you like the
smell of something in the oven.
The cords that bind your little bundle of self
have loosened. It's kind of like compassion."

The kid nearly misses his bus. I'm describing
hell's horrors: the burning sands,
the rotting carcasses on the beach, the people
drooling shit, the room of skeletons.
He is deciding not to drop acid this weekend.
Statius says, "Good boy," and reaches a
pseudopod over to pat the kid on the head in
benediction. It startles the kid.
He looks at me calmly ranting at nothing, leaps up,
and hurries away to catch his ride.

Canto XXII: Cheerios

At Statius' suggestion that "you stretch your legs
while still in possession of them," I've walked
towards where he says my appointment with Dante will be.
(Why act as if I believe him? Why not?)
The temples of conspicuous consumption that
lined the street have given way to
eating establishments. We're strolling by a
bright-lit place where people cheaply
fill their bellies while distracting themselves from the
food – that man at the corner table,

hunched behind his wall of rustling newsprint;
that female quartet, their salads half-finished,
leaning intently together over their sister's
woeful romantic tale and bursting
into raucous hoots and cackles – diners
glance their way, like beggars alert to
scraps thrown from the banquet; that unregarded
coffee cup askew on its saucer,
steam having ceased to rise long since from a surface
brown as floodwater, while he gazes

above it, seeking nourishment from Elsewhere.
"I enjoyed my last meal in

such a joint," says Statius, "It was a sugar
doughnut that I bought with a dollar I
bummed off a barmaid who knew me much too well.
I wasn't like these folks, I paid
attention of the utmost careful sort
to what I put in my body, and I
remember every sucrose crystal, how hard
and pointy it was until it melted

off my tongue. I don't believe I'd eaten
anything else for several days, and
lord! that lovely pastry refreshed the fire
in my middle scotch had lit all
morning. So I took my glow outside to
join it to the afternoon sun,
crossed the street to the vacant lot without
untoward incident. I
felt quite fit, and I was shocked when I looked
down to find the ground so close.

I was beyond surprise when it hit my nose.
I spread my arms and hugged the dirt,
dancing cheek to cheek with mother earth.
After a while they came and got me,
put me in a bed and plugged me with tubes, and
what with one thing and another –
cancer, pneumonia – there thankfully wasn't enough
fight left in me to make it last long."

Now, we're passing a glossy purple door
with graceful yellow cursive letters

painted above it and printed also on the
menu encased in glass beside it,
offering patrons a somewhat more elevated
set of choices of fare, at greatly
elevated tariffs, than those available
to the habitués of the humbler
eatery we were passing when Statius began his
distressing revelation, although the
clients of either café (as both are styled) might
equally be inclined to narrow the

list to "The Regular." "Thankfully?" I ask.
He answers, "Oh, hell yes. Death is
not so bad, but dying's a bitch. But I was
thankful for more than release from that.
Don't get me wrong. If it wasn't for Mahler, and birdsong,
and any one of a dozen women
for whom I enjoyed the sweetness of hopeless longing,
and most of all the magic of language,
I'd have checked out long before. Language!
It's what drew me to you, my friend.

I love a man of letters. What I could not
hardly abide was just the finger
lickin' heapin' helpings each day brings of

grind grind grind grind grind. The crunch of
burnt toast. The crunch of tires on gravel.
The crunch of broken bar glass.
The crunch of – well, if I said dreams, as I
was going to say, I'd be a liar;
dreams don't crunch. It's everything else does,
mostly. A body gets tired of the noise, the

visible darkness, the useless uses, weary,
stale, and flat as day old beer.
When that white-smocked doctor pronounced me, like he
was death's busboy clearing my plate and
asking did I want to see the dessert cart,
I'd have kissed the dear man if I
could have moved my lips. Free at last!
Free at last! Praise the lord, I'm
free at last! You know, the medics kept saying,
drink'll kill you; my momma and poppa

prayed that I'd get shut of that demon rum.
But, if wonder were in me, I'd wonder:
could I have lasted as long as I did without –
you know, you get in bed and light
a candle at your feet and drink sweet bourbon
'til you see two candles; cures
the common cold, and I was uncommonly cold.
Oh, hogwash! Who am I kidding?
I had best not lie to you, or I'll never

get to heaven! Truth is, I was

through and through a boozer. The day I surrendered,
born again in that amber river, I
took a long deep breath right there on that bar stool,
said to myself, *Self, you'd last a
whole lot longer being a Friend of Bill but
then you'd be a stranger to me*, and
that was the sweetest and bitterest shot of them all."
Here, they're never open for lunch.
At dinnertime, people will converse politely
over artfully plated comestibles:

roulades de boeuf en croute, thai scented aspic,
chipotle seared mahi mahi with
remoulade des kiwis et ananas,
paired from an extensive wine list
with whatever the bartender finds convenient,
and, to end with, the locally famous
endive sorbet. So says a snippet affixed to the
doorpost, where I direct my eyes while
at a loss for words. But Statius supplies them.
He says, "What you want to know is,

why am I up here, alongside you all,
when I should by rights be plunked down
mute and tangled in that thorny thicket
where self-slaughterers are set aside,

pickling my roots and feeling no pain?" His voice
assumes a pitch and intonation
higher, like the Florentine's. "Your error
is to think the self is something
unitary and durable, which it is
not, and not the congeries of

temporarily associated
processes that it is." He shivers;
that is, all his pieces quiver at once, like
aspen leaves quaking in the wind.
"Something came over me." His voice is his.
"I think your friend is drawing nigh.
Anyway, yes, I'm hither and I'm yon. And
I owe him – your friend, I mean –
a debt of gratitude I'll never repay.
It was a line of his I read, too

late to yank me back from where I was going, but
just in time to open my eyes to
where I had been. It may not seem like much:
First comes vision, and then, love.
When I read that, the morning of my last
waltz, a fire ran up my spine, and I
knew that until then I'd had it backwards. And –
poof! It was like the breath of god,
animating these few sorry bits to
want to try again. Oh, glory!"

He falls quiet. Then, musingly: "Strange: the
fortunate state in which you find me; the
dismal mangroves' brittle numbness; my former
confusions; discontinuous, separate.
Ego evaporates; the flame goes out.
And yet, I remember everything."
We're passing by a little park with a weeping
willow. Beneath its umbrella, a gentle
voice, a coo, a woman sitting on a
bench gives cheerios to her baby.

Canto XXIII: Swallow

We cross a parking lot packed with SUVs,
row upon row of shiny blocks,
solid as bullocks, puissant, well-padded inside,
resting between bouts of guzzling.
Their passengers throng that long, low building,
supporting the plastic bag industry.
Statius says our path leads through its aisles; a
kindred spirit will greet us there. When
I ask who, he's coy, and to my hopeful
ears the curlicues of tone

adorning his words, like ribbons on a package,
hold back a sweet surprise – my guide?
My sweet lost spring of love, refreshed? I follow
through the double sliding plate glass
doors and to the right past the rank of cashiers
to Produce, where an elderly woman
inspects potatoes. She picks one up with thumb and
forefinger, holds it high before her
eyes to catch the light, and turns it this way,
that way, peering suspiciously at it,

then returns it to the bin and rummages
roughly after one more perfect.

"Not her. It's someone you know. Or knew," says Statius.
Is it the family in the next aisle?
Her hair as wild as solar flares, the little
girl received her first tooth fairy's
visit just last night. Crying because her
mommy will not let her use her
tooth fairy money to buy chocolate pudding, she
clings to the shopping cart. Her brother,

fuzzy from a get-rid-of-the-lice shave,
clings to the opposite side of the cart and
sings a song he knows annoys her. Their elder
brother (sworn to secrecy on the
matter of fairies) sulks behind their mother,
angry because if those two twerps
make mom mad there'll be no pizza tonight.
In faded yellow cotton sundress,
skinny twenty-something mother bites her
lower lip. She pulls the usual

brightly labeled box off the shelf with barely a
conscious thought and tosses it into her
basket, her arm so near to following through with a
whack at junior it hurts not to.
She remembers when she was little, and something
hollow opens in her stomach.
She says, "Who wants to help me choose a pizza?"
I don't know any of these people.

Others I don't know include the chunky
blonde enjoying the coolness the dairy case

breathes at her while she deliberates
among the fat free yoghurts she
believes will help her lose those final pesky
pounds, and near her, the nervous brunette
consulting on her cell phone with her boyfriend
concerning: cream, or half and half?
He'll get mad if she brings home the wrong one.
There's also the pear-shaped man in the meats,
applying to the selection of a sirloin
exacting standards of color and shape.

The steak he chooses was hacked from a downer cow.
Further down, two college boys are
cramming a cart with cases of social lubricant,
gallons of high fructose corn
syrup beverages, chips, and fistfuls of jerky.
I pick up a plastic tub
containing more high fructose corn syrup,
water, plain old corn syrup,
coconut oil and palm kernel oil,
sodium caseinate from milk,

flavorings natural and artificial, modified
food starch, gum of xanthan and gum of
guar, polysorbate, polyphosphates,

sorbitan monostearate, and beta
carotene "for color". The label's blue and the
contents are white as Moby Dick.
I've eaten them often. Familiar, too, the voice
now saying, "Buddy, watch your step,
you almost disrupted my personal integrity,
or what remains of it." I halt.

A huge man, pale-faced, whose thick lips smile
beneath a mushroom cap of wild,
black hair so long it almost hides his eyes,
watches me reshelve the package.
"Swallow! What are you doing here?" I say.
He died five years ago. I turn
to Statius, say, "It's not who I expected."
"Disappointed?" Swallow asks, still
smiling. I say, "Yes, but not unhappy.
All our times together, making

ourselves stupid, getting midnight munchies!
It was a taste of brotherhood.
I feared I might have found you some place lower."
"I kicked the weed in time to move
beyond it. Hey, here comes Potato Lady.
She's giving you the hairy eyeball!
Who does she think you're talking to? I love to
hang out here, at our favorite aisle:
chocolate chip cookies, Little Debbies,

sour cream and onion flavored

Pringle chips, tortilla chips, baked pretzels,
Cheez Whiz, Screaming Yellow Zonkers,
I could go on and on. I watch the people
feeding appetites that have nothing to
do with food. Comfort? Mmmm. Safety?
Stretch your belly. Spirituality?
Chew, chew, chew. Nourishment?
Fuggedaboutit. They've forgotten
what food is and where it comes from and why
their maws can't get no satisfaction,

tomatoes that taste as sweet as wet pussy,
where an egg slips from, how hot the
blood is spurting from the pig's slit throat.
The fatter they get, the emptier they are.
The only thing you won't see on that list
of crap they use to crap that crap
you glop on your genetically-manipulated,
firm-for-longer-storage, reeking-of-
eighteen-wheelers'-diesel, cardboard-flavored,
spotless, glistening, blemish-free and

looks-just-like-the-picture strawberries, is a
moral choice. It's like the books and
magazines they sell here: glossy, pumped up,
dumbed down, pretend. Tits and Ass.

Ten Tricks to Drive Him Wild. Your Butt's Too Big."
"You're working on disgust?" I ask.
"Damn straight," he says, "my tool of liberation.
But what about you? I might ask you
just what you're doing here, all tight within
your skin but loose enough upstairs

to hang with the likes of me. Now, that's some trip!
I wish I'd known about that shit
back when it might have done me any good."
No psycho-social self-medication
brought me here, I tell him: rather, something
stranger by far and far more lasting:
I was sent for, the message carried to me
by that poet for whom love was the
power that moved the sun and the other stars,
from a blinked out love of mine.

Canto XXIV: We Leave the House of Gluttony

"Good story, bro. You know, I know your guy."
When we were teenage hippies together,
appalling suburbia's straights, Swallow's signature
trope was the topper. Got a hot rod?
Swallow's cousin's Vee-dub's got a Porsche
beneath the bonnet, will blow by a
statie like he's standing still. Smoke some
righteous dope? Swallow had some
one toke Afghan Black, it tripped him
out for half a week. And so on.

Now, he unreels a highly colored string of
circumstance that never quite
extends so far as to make the promised connection:
Swallow, same as ever. Statius
and I listen, interjecting just
enough to keep the words unwinding.
We're as charmed as if he were serving us cupcakes.
"Delicious," we signal, and "bring another."
He does, through many looping, loopy courses.
At last, satiated, Statius

breaks in. "Fellow pilgrim, that was the nicest
rant I've heard since moving to my

present digs. You're right; we're on the
lookout for that soul who stands
above all modern poets like a sentinel
tree in the middle of the waste – or,
to be kinder, the middle of a meadow,
spiring over the little flowers and
grasses, not another like him for miles."
I think he's pushing it a bit,

but Statius doesn't know the guy like I do.
He doesn't know dear Swallow, either.
I can tell the big man's getting set to
best Statius in superlatives.
"We would have a different poetry, if we
went to him to learn what he teaches,"
I say. Statius answers, "But the professors have
laid their claim and fenced him off.
Nobody goes near him without they've got a
string of letters after their name.

Heck, it's worse than that! Back when poets were
busting free of romanticism's
toxic detritus, and modernism swept the
field like kudzu overgrowing a
landfill, who were chief among his champions?
Smart-snob bully-boys Ezra Pound and
Tough Shit Eliot! Might as well have mounted
guards outside the bookstore armed with

shotguns warning off the common folk –
you're too dumb for this! So, now the

unwashed shoot us poets all the bird, say,
*Yeah, forget y'all, you're boring
and annoying.* They've buried the heart of it under
weedy blankets of mindy thinkings.
What's left over? The curdled narcissism –"
"Ill-digested aperçus!"
"– and overcooked verbiage," he continues, ignoring
my humble contribution,
"they belch out on nearly every page of
APR and *Poetry.*"

"...with a nice side of word salad?"
Swallow offers, to prove that he can
play this game, too. While Statius considers
(if cognitive processes may be ascribed
to men, however surprisingly competitive,
who are dead) whether this gambit
may be accepted as that of sort of an equal,
I ask Swallow if he remembers our
summer at the commune, organic gardening:
the semi-decrepit farmhouse four

of us (plus girlfriends on weekends) shared; the sunny
plot we weeded and watered by hand;
the secret "cash crop" planted a disavowable

distance from the house at a seldom
visited clearing in the woods; the woodchuck that
devastated our bush beans; the crooked
barreled .22 we'd almost decided
would be better used as a club when
Ralph got lucky and shot the beast; our silent
consensus that having killed it we had to

eat it; the stew, with our tomatoes and onions;
the black day that Swallow discovered
black fungus had devoured the cash crop;
the boxes of shiny zucchini, tomatoes,
cabbages, acorn squash, and root vegetables
(beets and carrots) we disciples of
Rodale left some clumps of dark, rich dirt on;
the proud day we toted boxes
of produce up the food co-op's aisles
instead of dropping them off at the back

(we might have swaggered if they weren't so heavy)
and collected the hundred seventy
three dollars that were our summer's earnings.
Of course he remembers. It was the most
important summer of his life, until then!
It turned him to farming! We reminisce.
Statius jumps in: "Someone's behind you," he says.
I look around and interrupt
a tall, young man in the act of reaching his hand

to pat my shoulder. He's magnificent

in his scarlet blazer with gold piping,
navy blue dress chinos, flat top
fringe of pale red hair, pale eyes, pale cheeks, a
glisten of dew on his long upper lip
betraying his nerves. Behind him, arms crossed, clutching a
box to her chest as if it were a
baby, stands the grim-faced Potato Lady.
Hastily pulling his hand back, he says,
"Sir, I have to ask you to leave the store,"
his voice pitched higher than he wanted.

For an instant I regret not letting his
hand pass through the cloud of me, but
I'm not here to indulge in the satisfactions
of malicious ghosts. I say,
"Okay, I'll go. This place is haunted. Creepy."
I give two big stage winks – to Swallow
on my right and Statius on my left – and,
striding past Potato Lady,
glimpse the label on her box: "***Sweet!***
New Style Instant Mashed."

Canto XXV: Red Jacket

Red Jacket ushers us through the stock room
out the loading dock door,
down a brief flight of concrete steps and
onto asphalt, its black flecked with
white sparkles in the midafternoon sun.
"Why," I ask, "do you hang back?"
"You talking to me?" asks Swallow, still perched atop
the laminated rubber bumper,
a constellation of holographic rainbows
the sun, behind him, shimmers through.

And then he's gone and it stings my unshielded eyes.
Until that final fadeout, he was
almost scarily Swallow as I remembered him.
Statius speaks up. "I'm in communion
with our Italian friend, whose dissipation –
spatial spread, I mean, like peanut
butter on warm toast – that is, released from the
multi-layered biochemical
and whatever bonds of life – I cast no
moral aspersions, you understand –

our fringes overlap – though, for me,
'dissipation' is the *mot juste* – "

"Pull yourself together and say what you mean."
Red Jacket appears to be pondering
whether my last remarks were addressed to him, and
if so, whether it would be wise to
offer a reply, but Statius continues:
"Ahem... Our friend says like you, he was
troubled by what he perceived of those who'd passed on.
He demanded his guide explain

how their condition could be so different and
so much the same as when they lived.
*Statius, he says, tell him what they told me.
that it may be a comfort to him.*"
The disquisition that follows, I struggle so hard
to understand, I hardly remember it.
Something about the veins of our bodies, branching
as fine as sprays of baby's breath,
carrying blood and with it animating
"perfect blood" that burns in the limbs

and unconsumed descends to places a medieval
Christian might be ashamed to name
and in a man turns pale as louched absinthe,
in a woman lushly red.
The sperm falls on the menstrual blood in the womb
like rennet into milk, he says.
"There coagulates a homunculus."
Once the brain's articulated

fully and precisely, "god breathes on it."
"Statius," I say, "hold on," but he

continues, deadpan, deadly serious. "Here's
the really important part," he says.
Something about the breath of god combining
with the active and passive principles
already present, like sunlight giving warmth to
mashed grapes brings forth wine, and the
brain is "raised to a higher state." (I snigger;
he ignores it.) Formerly dumb as a
sea cucumber, now it possesses reason.
"Here's the important part," he says.

Like wine, that to a subtle and knowing palate
reveals its own "tear war" – "What?!" –
"The character of its native soil – *terroir*!" –
so each sentient being is stamped with the
circumstances of its making. Losing
the corporeal, what is left
impresses itself on the air like a lingering scent.
A lengthy pause. "It's beautiful. Mostly.
The parts I get. But not much help," I say.
"It's useless because it's bullshit," he says.

"Why did you tell me, if you don't believe it?"
"I'm dead. I don't believe in anything.
What was it Whitman said – *the unseen is proved by the*

*seen, 'til that becomes unseen and
receives proof in its turn.* Well, maybe.
Y'all look mostly the same to me.
I told you because he wanted me to: loving
him I honored his desire."
"You love?! And he desires?!" "I did, with affection
so much of a piece with me

you might say it was part of my *tear war*.
Being myself an ardent spirit,
I like the idea that life's long fermentation
locks in us some unique patterns
traceable when they're sensed by connoisseurs.
And he, of course, would not have written
what he did not want for you to know."
"So, love and desire outlast death?"
"You want to hear something simple, like yes or no.
That lovely medieval embryological

fairy story, you want something like that, only
couched in language you've learned from science
because they've taught you when they peel back cell walls
and go poking among the squiggles,
the breath of god is one thing they don't find.
A cosmic orphan's fear of endings –
it's right there, so strong! in your *tear war*."
After a pause through which he outlasts me,
I venture, "If you had eyes, you'd see right through me,"

"If I had a head, I'd nod,"

he says, nodding the part where a head would be,
"but I digress. When I said you
were taught, I didn't mean just books in school.
We baby boomers, aptly named,
were born after Oppenheimer's apotheosis
that early dawn of July 16,
1945, near Alamogordo.
He said to himself – and it was true –
Now I am become Shiva, destroyer of worlds.
But Shiva has many faces and names:

Truman, Eisenhower, John Fitzgerald
Kennedy, Lyndon Johnson, Tricky
Dick Nixon, Jerry Ford, Jimmy
Carter, Reagan, Clinton, Bush,
Josef Djugashvili, Malenkov, Nikita
Krushchev, Leonid Brezhnev, Yuri
Andropov, Konstantin Chernenko, Mikhail
Gorbachev, Yeltsin, Putin. We were
born to a world ruled by lords of death
whose potency any instant might

be subject to the strictest verification.
You learned from them where to look for
ultimate answers. The flavor of bullshit you want
me to give you comfort with has

words like *quantum mechanical* this or that,
dark energy and matter
rising out of *Dirac's Sea,* just like a
huge and unexplorable continent;
you want I should say, *ninety percent
of all that is, is something y'all*

*know sweet fuck-all about: go look for your
immortal soul over there.* But
half understood technical terms are mighty
thin protection against the cold, and
at the heart of physics is uncertainty,
just where Gödel proved it should be.
Maybe, maybe, maybe, maybe, maybe...
What does a poet have to offer
in the face of all this that is not
merely charming or otherwise false?

I never knew for sure. Still, as the blues
song says, *I can't be satisfied
and I just can't keep from trying.* So try this on.
Whom do you wake up with, every morning?
Is it the same as whom you went to bed with?
Where'd that person go, last night,
while someone laid there in your body, dreaming?
Who dreamed there, the night before?
Where'd that person go, in the space between dreams?
Who was it who drew your breaths?

The voices of your father and mother sometimes
issue from your lips. Your lover's
trembling as you enter echoes under
your skin. Your teacher's thoughts
become your own. Your steps lengthen to match
the stride of an absent friend. A stranger's
actions sometimes turn out to have been yours.
What have they in common? What,
but the mutual acquaintance of a living body?"
I'm still contemplating this when

Red Jacket, having watched me so long
rapt and showing no sign of moving,
vents his worry: "Sir, do you need help?"
I speak to the tiny part of him that's
not impatient and wants to know: "I'm fine,
my friend, and I'll be on my way."
"Not a moment too soon," says Statius, "Victoria's
waiting to meet you in the flesh."
I follow him, weaving through the car park's
heat devils into the shade of the trees.

Canto XXVI: Lust

Condoms litter the grove like skins depleted
of their fruits, the emblematic
debris of acts whose warmth is generated
mainly by friction and not sustained by
intimacy's nuclear reaction.
Teens' romantic scavenger hunts,
following clues derived from movies, music,
ads and observation of their
parents, found their sticky ends in these peels.
In brilliant spasms older men

obliterated a moment's loneliness and
left these husks their paid companions
wouldn't pick up, either. Alcoholic
trysts, soon forgotten, and the
memorable night that oriental chick, or
was she Jewish, pulled a train of
eagerly sheepish basketball players of whom
just one insisted on "protection,"
and –there beneath that Norway maple –
a newly enamored couple whose perfect

focus on each other rendered them blind to the

weedy squalor surrounding their lovemaking
until, awakening from a brief, sweet doze,
she shrieked with disgust to see what dangled
from a twig just inches above her forehead;
all have deposited evidence of their
passing passions. "Here's another thing
that takes a living body," I say,
and then, espying under a bush some wrinkled
pages bearing flesh-toned photos,

tokens the onanists also are represented
here, I add, "at least one body."
"That's more true than you might think," says Statius,
"but your Vic will clear it up." He
makes no move to move me on. I let the
sadness of this place, the gap
joy sags into between what is and
what is wished for, bleaken me.
Here lay the girl who wanted a baby to love her.
Here the boy lay, thrusting at manhood.

Here a woman played the easy robot.
Here a man felt masterful.
Here she did what she wanted, it doesn't matter.
Here his shame was drowned in shame.
Here she made damn sure she wasn't her mother.
Here he proved just what he was made of.
Here she let him do it so he'd love her.

Here he brailled wetness and thought he read "want."
Here she gauged her prettiness by his stiffness.
Here they all look the same in the dark.

Here she accepted her punishment, or fought it.
Here he was grateful for what she gave him.
Here her breasts were like flocks of cooing doves.
Here a six-pack formed his tummy.
Here she shuddered into a moment's escape.
Here he took his time upon her.
Here was something to do when she was bored.
Here he tended a private garden.
Here they experimented with cold fusion.
Here they closed their eyes on each other.

"Don't you feel the slightest churning burning
yearning, standing here?" asks Statius.
"No," I lie. The fact is, a subtle congestion is
not unpleasantly perceptible
in my groin, as if a cat were purring
somewhere down there. Statius cocks his
upper appendage. I'd swear he's raised an eyebrow.
He says, "We'd better move on, now.
Unless you want to stick around and see what
night time brings." "Only a little,"

I confess, fearful that an animal
nature not fully enough subdued

may be deemed fatal to my mission.
"Close enough for government work," says
Statius, leading me further into the copse.
Or is it a woods? What seemed a mere
arboreal border from the parking lot
reveals more depth the deeper we enter
along this winding, constricted, bumpy path
close-hemmed with underbrush, while Statius

tunefully propounds philosopher and
poet Willie Dixon's classic
meditation: "What make these men go crazy
when a woman wear her dress so
tight? *hmm... hmm... hmm... hmm...*
What make these men go crazy when a
woman wear her dress so tight? *hmm...
hmm... hmm... hmm...* Must be the
same old thing that makes the tom cats fight all
night... must be the same old thing that

makes a preacher throw his Bible down..."
bodiless *a cappella* preceding me
often far ahead and out of sight.
After so many jigs and jags, I
don't know how far we've been walking, and
after Statius has left off singing a
while, how long a time. Now a fainter
trace where feet have etched the duff

  down to dirt curves gracefully as a grass-blade
    to the right. Now a straighter

  side track shoots to the left; at the junction,
    indian pipes bow their pale heads.
   Now I see these woods are filigreed with
    littler tracks that intersect each
  other and this main stem Statius stays on.
    There, behind that white pine,
sunshine streaks through dappled tenebrousness onto
    spots of orange, canada lilies –
I can just make them out; and then, more glades,
  like jewels hanging suspended on light-shafts,

  like other people's ideas of heaven. Ahead,
    sometimes to the right and sometimes
    to the left depending on how the path
    elbows through the trees, is one
    particularly bright. At last, we burst
    into its glory of dandelions,
burdock, trampled grass and clover and violets,
    sprays of wild carrot, thistles,
  littered here as back at the trail's beginning.
   Maybe my mood has shifted. There,

  rut's discarded souvenirs seemed gross, but
    this sunny oasis seems graced by the
    wild tokens of profusion, boiling

from the ground prolific as mushrooms.
The cat that was purring in my groin has uncurled
itself, and stretches, yawning wide,
into a warmth throughout my torso. Statius,
pointing, tells me, "Look over yonder."
Across the clearing, a weathered brick wall.
In the wall, no windows, but

a door. Next to the door, a bronze plaque:
THROUGH ME YOU GO WHERE SORROWS GATHER
PAIN THAT ENDS IN NOTHING LEADS THROUGH ME
THROUGH ME YOU GO AMONG THE LOST
I AM BEYOND APPEAL OR JUSTIFICATION
POWER BEYOND YOUR POWER MADE ME
BEYOND KNOWING AT THE ROOTS OF LOVE
BEFORE ME ONLY THE LIVING WERE
FOREVER LET LOOSE HOPE AND THROUGH ME PASS
"Don't think you have to knock," says Statius.

Canto XXVII: The House of Loss

I feel I've come full circle, although I've never
been here before nor wished to be.
Statius says, "More like a spiral," and I
know I spoke the first part out loud.
He adds: "Dante's waiting through there, and that
woman child who gave you love."
I still don't move. He says, "You know, Victoria."
Behind me, the afternoon's late rays
stripe the glade; buzzing through them, a bee;
and far away, the human world.

Statius says, "I was a drunk and I
completed almost nothing it was
given me to do. It might could be my
own sad history of bogglement's
bugging me; but, I can't see why you would
waste so much of conscious life as
remains to you in standing stock still
outside this door that everybody's
got to go through in their own time, anyhow."
"I'm scared of what's within it!" I blurt.

So soothing and calm I hardly make out his words,
"Don't be a big baby," he says. I think,

if there's a white light, and he tells me
to go towards it, I'm going back.
My feet still fail me. "I am a big baby," I say.
He answers, "Maybe when you were all
fresh-sprung from hell, elated and ethereal,
maybe then you weren't ready.
But what have you been up to since, but coming
down to earth? Don't you want to

finally see your girl?" He's at my elbow,
a not too prickly nervous jangle
where his impulse joins and strengthens my own,
impelling me to reach for the knob and
grab and twist it. The door swings open smoothly,
immense weight in exquisite balance
pulling me into the vault. It takes some strength to
start it swinging shut behind me,
thudding upon this cool, dark room and its tenants.
They lie face up on metal carts

the size of picnic tables. I used to like
to lie on red-stained rough pine planks
and watch the clouds pass over my parents' yard
until I felt that I was moving,
not the clouds, and they were still as the bodies
that surround me into the dimness
in orderly rows extending in every direction.
I'm in the middle of the room

with no idea how I got there. Statius
startles me: "Do you know who's here?"

For answer, I begin to move among them.
Here's my father, that wise, strong man.
The last time that I saw him, he was dying.
"How are you?" I asked. "I'm pensive,"
he replied. Then, for several days,
he gazed at photos of his grandkids,
holding them up before himself like books.
When he was done, he replaced them carefully
on his bedside table, fell back to sleep, and
woke up only once, to die.

Here's my father's father, whom I last saw
clutched in anger's talons and calling
in a voice like grinding rocks. I
remember his shy, sweet smile,
the way his eyelids danced above it briefly
before becoming heavy again.
The year he died, my father saw him monthly.
After the last of those cross-country flights, I
asked was it hard to lose the old man. He said,
"He was gone long ago."

Here's my mother's father, the face of a wounded
hawk, high-cheekboned as any chief whose
image Edward Curtis preserved. He blessed my

childhood with boxes of onion-skin typescript,
reams of disorganized pages, essays and stories
full of force and urgency, wanting
only to be known but lost and mostly
unread, an Alexandrian library
I, through youthful indifference, casually sacked.
He was in a nursing home when

I last saw him, split in half by a stroke.
I told him that he was my hero.
"Don't you bullshit me," he said. His death
resulted from successful surgery;
he'd consented to having his sight restored, but
not to removal of his prostate.
His caregivers won that fight, and he stopped eating.
Here's my father's mother, who claimed her
grandchildren were her proudest, her only achievements,
having ruined her knees from kneeling on

wealthy people's kitchen floors to scrub them and
made a home and raised two sons.
Here's my mother's mother, little keeper
to the shadows, swept off her feet by a
hawk-faced force of nature and never able
to regain them. Women, shadowed.
Now I'm moving faster, seized by a sudden and
fiercening hope. Perhaps she's here!
Rushing from aisle to aisle (I hate to admit it),

rummaging through the siblings of cousins of

aunts of uncles of ancestors, friends – I halt when
Statius says, "You're looking for love in
all the wrong places. It takes a living body."
Where, in this cavernous hall of loss,
shall I find such a thing? A silvery swooping
line, as fine as spider silk,
appears in the darkness, running from my navel
to a distant cart. I follow.
On it: me. "*Tat tvam asi*," says Statius.
As I stare at it, it breathes.

Air seeps to the bottom of the lungs, then
lifts the sternum, then the space
beneath the collarbones expands and then it
contracts, the sternum falls, the diaphragm
shrinks, the cycle begins anew, a dozen
repetitions before I'm aware a
slight congestion in one nostril causes a
hiss as faint as the tie that binds us.
Fluids pump and trickle within and beneath the
pinkish, tough integument, carrying

all the goods and waste of cellular commerce.
In the guts' pale, writhing coils,
microorganisms tend their affairs.
The heart clenches and unclenches, the

beautiful sleek liver performs its chemical
transformations, inside the skull
layers of skeins of neurons flicker unceasingly.
Hair and fingernails keep growing.
Statius tells me I must lie down on it,
"head to head and toe to toe, and

then... let go, just let yourself sink in."
I hesitate, fearing pain, the horrid
discordant scramble of sensations I have
learned to expect from touching another
too deeply. He says, "You claimed you wanted to
meet, protect, and greet Victoria.
If you only want to see a shade, well,
stick around. There's millions of us.
Her, you'll find no way but through that body."
I lie down gingerly: not that bad,

at first, like coming back to somewhere you
can find your way in without light.
But now the muscles quiver, shake and tighten.
They cramp in knots that stab like fire!
"Gently," says Statius, "You want to be in possession,
not in a seizure. Breathe into it."
Terrified, desperate, I do. The agonies fade,
bit by bit. At last I rest in
harmony, hand in hand and heart in heart
in this my home, and open my eyes.

Canto XXVIII: The Earthly Paradise

"You're not the first who up and walked out of that
    particular kind of place." That's Statius,
        on the left. And Dante, on the right:
    "I give you my assurance, though you
    don't need it: on the day when Atropos shears
your thread, they'll take you back." He's smiling;
        I hear it. Blue, blue, blue in my eyes,
            blue as my father's the day he died,
blue as Katrina's over the Northshore that morning,
        clear and calm before my eyes.

    "Welcome to the earthly paradise," they
    chorus. A woodpecker's drumroll announces
        dinner – grubs again. A robin calls his
            pretty girl – pretty girl.
        Far away, a jay is yelling at something.
        Nearby, a dove's self-satisfied gurgle.
    I am quite content to lie here, listening,
        adding these ripples to the blue.
At the nape of my neck and the small of my back, my
        spine carries me off the ground

    in short hops. The back of my head, my shoulders,
        buttocks, calves and heels press dirt, my

arm and leg muscles loose as Dali clocks.
Air caresses the rims of my nostrils,
ebbs and floods in my lungs. Pebbles prick the
backs of my hands and blades of grass
between my fingers tickle them. The bowls of my
upturned palms fill with blue.
I am warm beneath the deep-piled blanket
Aeolus weaves. Its ever-shifting

warp and weft bring me a musk, sweet-sharp on a
base of long-dried sweat, unpleasant if
it were stronger, I recognize as my own.
A tannic streak of dry, baked
earth cuts sweet vegetable aromas
and the unmistakeable, rich,
heavy tang of fresh dog poop.
Dogshit in paradise? I think, then:
*Why not? This sphere contains all others – the
terror that leavens the boredom of hell, the*

*purgatorial twitch between pleasure and pain – this
central, peaceful awareness subsumes them.*
I don't know where this thought came from. It doesn't
feel like mine.I scratch an itch that's
suddenly sprung in my left ear lobe, yawn, and
in my long-unopened mouth a
taste of staleness blooms. I run my tongue
around my teeth, and stand, and stretch.

I've emerged from sleep surrounded by trees.
I somehow must have stumbled into

one of those clearings I saw as floating gems when
Statius led me through the woods, and
must have fallen, baring my face and heart to the
moon and stars and black of night, and
to this gentle morning's laving grace.
My face feels fresh and moist. I don't
know where these clothes came from. They smell fresh cleaned.
My arms, extending, mimic the trees
just as we did in preschool, and I laugh and am
glad to have greeted the day this way.

"This is the day, I am sure, that I will see her,"
I tell my companions. Dante answers,
"She is nearer than you might imagine."
But which of the winding, criss-crossing paths
that lace this woods will bring me the rest of the way?
I hesitate, filling with doubt. Once more,
Statius applies the goad: "For crying out loud, man!
Any way you go, she's there."
This clearing has four exits. The one to my left's
less littered with latex jetsam. I take it.

My shoulders feel the heavy shawl of sunlight
lift from them. A bit of pre-dawn
coolness lingers here. I amble, easy in

body and in mind. A maple
sapling strains straight skyward, towards a
window its elders' canopy left
open. Its leaves fan out above its peers,
tasting the sunlight they lean in to
capture, cramping and stunting its lower limbs.
On the edge of a glade, three paper

birches dance in a gentle, expanding spiral.
A black alder rises a thick,
columnar dozen feet, sign of a vigorous
youth now gnarled by burls, before it
splits four ways: one upthrusts another
forty diagonal feet, like an arm
raised in defiance but bearing instead of a fist a
squirrel nest atop its greenery;
one writhes more-or-less horizontally a
similar distance; the third limb's rising

arc is just too full of elbows to be
graceful; the fourth branch is absent, a
white, smooth, barkless stump marking
where it fractured off the bole.
Most of the trees are dappled with lichen colonies,
crusty or leafy or like wee shrubs,
algae and fungi conjoined in patches of greys or
yellows or greens. Shelves of polypores
ornament the aging and unhealthy.

Over there, the duff's a-bubbling with

chanterelles, gold on brown, variations
on a wrinkled and trumpet-shaped theme.
Underfoot, roothairs and mycelia
knit a filamentary network
pulsing with commerce in carbon, water and nitrogen
from each according to ability,
to each according to its need. My soles,
unshod as Moses, read the ticker.
Within a step or two, all of this registers
on my senses, and more: foliage

riddled with caterpillars' scallop-edged holes and
beetles' ragged lacerations,
torn by grasshoppers, gnawed by sawflies
down to a delicate lace of veins,
bumpy with warty and nipple-shaped galls full of eggs,
folded into tents by spiders.
Insects skitter over and in and under
flowers and ferns and blades of grass!
The letters newts and salamanders carve in air, the grunt of a toad,
the birds!

Squirrels bark, as rough as bark! I'm whelmed.
Whelming's overcoming me.
If this is paradise, to be wholly here, then
it's too much, like being inside an

imploding piñata, like drowning, like being swept up
in a tornado, much too much to
handle, darkening like an iris dissolve.
In almost my voice comes the saving thought:
*Consciousness preserves itself by controlled
obnubilatory metonymization.*

An orange newt is frozen on a rock
by my left foot. Bending low,
I look it in the eye. It runs. It's gone.
I know the fallen pine it's under
harbors also a quiet metropolis of
grubs and beetles, molds and worms, but
I don't have to pay attention if I don't
want to. I'm master of my will.
Each sound rests on stillness like a jewel.
White to black, each zone holds detail.

Reveling in multiplicity,
I wander, focusing near or far,
throughout the woods or on a moth's antenna,
learning by whim and by perseverance.
What I'm learning, I can't say. I'm learning
what I can't say. Hours later
finds me staring up a smooth, grey fountain,
trying to tighten vocabulary
around it, like a slipping pipe-wrench that if you
tighten it too much crimps the pipe.

Words are either too loose or procrustean.
Something long, dark brown and curly
catches my eye. It's "hair." A "woman's" "hair." She's
sitting on a fallen branch at the
base of this giant "elm" I've been absorbed by,
cross-legged, head cocked left, and smiling
at me as I finally come around. She's
humming Stephen Foster's *Hard Times*
in a clear contralto, but stops when I think this.
"I see you've met the trees," she says.

Canto XXIX: Off the Wheel

Somewhere within the possible patterns among the
hundred trillion synapses my brain
brings to greet her hundred trillion are all the
ways a man might respond to a beautiful
woman sitting on a tree branch deep in a
forest when she affably greets him.
How on earth do I narrow it down to one?
Experience is no guide, and both my
guides are silent. I could be as befuddled
as the teenager I was in the

purgatorial 'sixties, picking his way through the
rubble of a collapsing culture – the
Dating Emporium now an open field, the
stalls that stabled the Sex Role Models
wrenched all gappy and leaning crazily, the
Gender Norms blown loose from their
containers, shattered and scattered far and wide – his
ears popping in the vacuum that
hubbed a whirlwind of contending voices.
Happily, I'm in paradise, now.

"Come with me," she says, and unfolds herself to
stand before her perch, and offers her

arm – I take it – and so we promenade through the
underbrush. I rest my hand in the
warmth of her elbow and take her lead. She says,
"Nothing like walking for bringing a person
back from over exertions of the spirit.
I would like to show you something,
when you're ready. That may be a while.
You've come so far, unnaturally fast."

Nothing will nourish the spirit like being seen, and
nothing so much as being seen with a
loving regard. Eager for more such food, I
lay my recent adventures before her.
Maybe this easy, whole-hearted, knowing welcome
from a stranger seems strange to you.
To me, in paradise, it seems no stranger than
what met me a week ago.
I was walking home in high good humor.
Just that morning I had received an

unexpected kindness, and unexpected
money had arrived in the mail that
afternoon, and so I bestowed my smile on
traffic and birds and weeds alike, on a
college kid eating a hoagie on his stoop, on a
squash plant fruitfully multiplying, on
two little children, a fat tabby sunning, a
stern-faced woman jogging towards me,

knees up, hands curled into loose fists,
horizontal forearms pistoning

straight back and forth, torso encased in
orange petroleum products. The only
bouncing thing about her was her hair,
black and wavy, freely framing a
narrow, swarthy face whose whole expression
rested in the olive eyes, that
strange and distant look of a serious runner,
until they caught my happy glance and her
lips twisted into a scowl or grimace – her
answer to a smiling man.

Oh, the strangeness we swim in, unconscious as fish!
I share these thoughts with my new friend.
Her reply is a flick of the skirt and a flash of the
blade she carries to ward off evil, "for
closing the door on them in hell," as she puts it.
"Have you, uh, slammed some doors?" I ask.
"I don't walk these woods at night, and I'm a
peace-loving girl from Ohio, but one day
not too far from here, I was offered a
choice that was no choice: to suffer

and be still, or not to be still, and suffer.
I chose the latter... and he was still."
She pats my hand that rests in the crook of her arm.

"Happily, you're in paradise."
Her pinky finger's missing its distal phalange.
I decide not to ask her about it.
She is at ease with my silence, and neither Dante
nor Statius sounds an alarm, so I
digest her confession – if that is what it is – and
slowly my comfort matches hers.

This warrior spirit poses no danger to me.
We proceed as companionably and
quietly as the oldest of friends. Now she
draws my attention to a flower or
toad or shift of light she thinks I might like, and
I respond in kind; she teases
me about my "cheap brown getting-released-
from prison suit;" I compliment
her on her flowing linens; and we enter a
conversation that places us vividly

in relation to each other, here,
perfect and in proportion like figures
strolling through a Chinese landscape painting.
I'm not sure about her, but I am
no less human for being in paradise, which
is to say a verbal monkey,
so, as with accumulating details
she enlargens to fill my frame of
perception, I begin to imagine what's hidden

besides that knife beneath her skirt.

It comes as something of a relief, then, when
she says, "We're almost there," and stops
engaging with me quite so personally,
drawing me forward with greater urgency.
Not long after, the trees abruptly release us
into an immense green space much
like the quadrangular emptiness at the heart of our
nation's capitol, minus the tiny
encroaching memorials and collections of stuff
our leaders try to fill it with,

and twice as broad. Two-thirds its length from here,
a ferris wheel tall as a double rainbow
haltlingly cycles boxcar-sized gondolas. CHILDREN
UNDER TEN ARE NOT ADMITTED,
announces a sign by one of its mammoth stanchions.
The line for it snakes to us, almost.
"Watch them ride," she says, her hand in mine.
They start out chatting happily,
maybe a little nervous anticipation
speeding that first step off the ground

into the swinging, crowded iron contraption.
Up and out and up and out, and
by the time it turns to up and in and
up and in, the cheer is crusting over, the

good expansive thrill of rising within a
common roof by slow degrees amid
ever more distant horizons has rotted with anxious
misgivings and fear. Somewhere, someone
shoved someone, someone grabbed someone's
something, someone's someone slept with

someone, sides were taken, factions split like
river ice in springtime and showered
words like blows and blows as prolific as words.
There's a long pause at the apex while
far below them newcomers hop-step aboard.
Up there, smooth-cheeked Cherubino,
remembering how he trilled with delight to be
run through by love, hears his voice break
against the judgment that banishes him for his wildness
to curdle in exile among the killers;

Montague lies with Capulet; Maria
cradles Tony's lifeless body;
few allow their eyes to stray out the uplifted
cabin's windows, and mostly not in
wonder but desperately seeking some way to escape.
On the descent, Remorse and Regret
put in appearances, and their far more numerous
dirty cousins Guilt and Shame, whose
snot-nosed couplings in dark corners spawn that
rampant brat, Self-Justification, who

shouts down all the others. Hushed, abashed,
fatigued, avoiding eye contact,
they welcome Harmony's tight-assed semblance, Order,
just as the car jolts to the ground.
Out the side the new arrivals are blind to, they
toss the corpses; as if to recapture the
Golden Age of their own first coming, they fête the
incoming innocents at the other.
Once in a long while, a figure walks
out of a car's grisly portal and

wanders alone, shaking, pale and thoughtful,
until it encounters another such, of
whom a few are dotted around the field, and is
greeted, perhaps with the brush of a palm to the
cheek, a gentle, cupping touch whose warmth is
felt before the skin meets skin, and the
shaking stops. They stand and talk in groups of
two or three or four like friends
sharing reluctance to part before all is shared.
At last, one shrugs – her time to go.

Final hugs exchanged, they watch her walk
not looking back to join the queue.
As the herd lines up behind her, she
remains an island of meditation
surrounded by eagerness, inching forward. Attendants,

sharp as razor wire, usher her
in among the survivors and slam the door.
"On the cars they ride, more faces
press to the glass at the top of the cycle, and fewer
bodies are thrown to mound on the grass."

Canto XXX: The Bug-eyed Gardener

    Her valedictory tone invites me to leave off
      gawking towards the wheel and to cast
    awareness freshly relaxed around the field.
     The first thing I look at, grateful, is her.
     I was drowning in a flood of unfiltered
    perceptions, when she found me. With a
   gifted teacher's skill, she led me through the
      labor of learning to ride that river,
     her wisdom guiding my apprehension,
       rib and plank, to form my craft.

     A baby, looking to its mother, hopes
      to find her eyes are feasting on it,
     so that it may feast on her attention.
      An adolescent hopes his eyes
    will join the eyes of the object of his hopes
      above a table laid with themselves.
   The infant and youth in me are disappointed.
    Her gaze turns wide to the glebe. Eager
    to see whatever she sees, I follow suit,
     scanning the joyful distance between

me and that rotating prison, glad to be furloughed, if
        only for this day. There,

far across the open field, is Statius,
queuing up to ride again.
Maybe he feels my eyes upon his back;
he turns and waves. It's like a tiny
flock of multi-colored starlings wheeling.
Someone who did not know him might see his
grace and gallantry and read it as cheery.
I watch him a while, wishing him well,

awash in a complex eddy of emotions.
Goodbye, dear friend. Unconsciously
at first, my eye wanders from him along
the line, and then, my interest captured,
skips about among the scattered clusters
hanging back from rejoining the throng,
pausing at faces of special beauty or strength
until, preceding by a second
the recognition of what it has lit upon,
a cold shock seizes me.

I glimpse hair like a heavy sheet of cornsilk.
It frames a thin, pale face,
hidden intermittently by the bulk of the
person between us, to her left.
Like an infant an adult subjects to a
"game" of peekaboo, I'm anxious
what has been obscured might have been absconded,
thrilled when sight confirms her presence.

I stumble forward, then walk smoothly as if to
keep from spilling a brimming bowl, and

in a time that has no time, I reach her.
I remember her girlhood's quicksilver
laughter, quiver-lipped sensitivity, her
volatile gay or sad abandon; but
now the woman steps between her friends (they
move aside like wings unfolding)
her features set and expressionless, just like
a judge about to take evidence.
"Dear heart," I say, "you once described yourself
to me as 'unafraid of words.'

Let me tell you how I learned I'd lost you.
I was coming home from somewhere.
It was a sunny August afternoon. Our
year in Europe was one year past.
If I got a number high enough in
Mister Nixon's lottery, I'd
drive cross country next year and at long last
lie beside you, skin to skin.
Otherwise, I'd have to go to college.
Maybe I was thinking about that,

trudging up the driveway. My mom leaned out the
door and called me: 'Somebody called just
now and said that Vicky died in a car crash.'

Just those words. Nothing more.
Not long after school had ended that summer,
the summer after the summer after
the Summer of Love, my friend Swallow'd said,
'Hold out your hand,' and in my palm
he'd placed a twist of paper filled with leaves.
More carefully instructed by

my wise friend Swallow in the art of toking
than I ever would be taught by
anyone to grieve – 'Take a deep hit.
Hold it. Hold it. Let it out.' –
I'd taken it home and lit it up, upstairs
in the bathroom, window open, towel
laid on the floor to seal the door crack. Then,
after spritzing half a can of
air refreshener, I had ventured forth
into a brighter, gigglier world.

It might have been nothing but an amusement, except
that day there was no future
with you in it. And the days that followed,
filled with smoke. Where you had been." That
night we'd said our private and last goodbyes, she'd
lolled on the bed like a cat that wants its
belly rubbed; but I had not yet learned my
way around the roadblocks an
adult had placed on the way to those pleasures

as if to mark the site as hers.

So, we'd talked, restlessly, trembling near an
unacknowledged brink until
our only choice was plunge or back off
and I, pleading the hour, left.
I continue: "With you, I first ventured
past simple friendship into...
well, I poked my head through a garden gate.
Timidly, yes, and bug-eyed with wonder!
Gone in a puff. And yes the dreary story:
marijuana became my refuge,

safe in my comfy bean chair, where good pizza and
Bach's Toccata and Fugue in D
equally absorbed attention, so much like
heaven you'd think it was next door and
not a million miles away. And though I
learned the enjoyment of sex and even to
call it 'making love' sincerely, that place we'd
tiptoed into, that fresh sweet
riot of intimate textures and fragrances you don't
even have to touch to feel

almost unbearably – that remained with you.
In a recurring dream, I couldn't
find the key to my locker – my high school locker.
Did you send it?" Yes, she nods.

"But, I didn't take the hint. I searched in
all the recommended, time-
honored, wrong venues – philosophy, history,
politics, mysticism, sex and
drugs and rock and roll. I tended to fall for
inaccessible beauties – like you,

off limits! Having been ejected
once, so harshly, from that garden
you and I had sweetly stumbled into,
I was filled with awful horror
at the merest chance of setting foot
upon those paths again. And so I
stayed away from there as if it were guarded by
giant angels with flaming swords. I
clung to those who held me outside." I stop.
A muscle in her cheek has quivered.

Canto XXXI: The Song of Grief

"What are we to make of this sorry story?"
Victoria's gaze holds steady on me.
The voice is that of her who brought me here
from among the trees. "Drunks and addicts
always apologize; they feel downright awful;
they would have you pity the devil.
They have learned that saying, 'Sorry,' makes things
go away and piles up so much
comfy regret for them to smother themselves with.
Mister, is that all you've got?"

I cannot look away from Victoria's lovely
eyes' wet gloss, her fine-pored skin, the
grave expression she wears, so rare, for her.
"I'm not either of those," I say,
"I dulled a pain. I hid from what had hurt me.
I survived the best I knew how: a
trapped beast gnawing off its leg."
"Good. You've got some fight left in you.
But now you're in that place where nothing's hidden.
Tell us, Lover Man, what ended

for you in that car crash?" Pause. I think,
that zit you had on your chin has cleared up.

*We were sitting on the stairs outside your
mom's apartment, huddled together,
my arm and your arm crushed between us, fingers
enlaced between our thighs. Just a
few days left before we'd say good-bye.
I say, 'Where are Kate and Tony?'
as if either of us cared. Head bowed
as if speaking to your knees,*

*you say, 'I think they went somewhere else.
She's probably all over him.'
Your desire and wistful resignation, the
woman struggling with the not yet
outgrown nice girl, fill the stairwell potent
as crushed lavender and patchouli,
so strong! I am paralyzed.
Approaching voices break the spell.*
Playful, bright and sharp as a blade, the voice
breaks in: "Hold that thought.

What do you think your memories consist of?
Are they preserved like little marks in a
more or less carefully organized ledger, photos
stuck in appropriate places with
invisible tape? Digital video clips that
you can run by clicking the links?
Scratch-and-sniff panels? Audio files? Is there
in your head a little librarian

running around, filing and retrieving
metaphoric data caches?

Is that all you thought was left of her?"
"I had this thought that it might be
a mistake or a misunderstanding, a doubt
almost unconscious as breathing: she might be
somewhere out there." "How sweet! And how you
look straight in her eyes and say that!
Are you evoking a mystic communion of spirits?
Vibrating ectoplasmic essences,
resonating as one? Cupid's arrow
eternally pinning your two hearts?

Or some such twaddle. You know better, don't you?
If you'd listened in school, you would have
learned a psychology firmly grounded in sodium
ions, neural electric potentials and
firing patterns, transmitters and receptors,
serotonin, dopamine, and
most germane to love – oxytocin!
There's no inner homunculus rummaging
evidence boxes and files for affidavits
swearing her palms were sweating like yours.

It was *her* emotion you remembered!
What you recall of *her* is physically
part of *you*. If she lowered her eyes, the

nerves behind your eyes would fire as
if to lower your eyes, too, and if her
voice grew softer, you could feel it
in your throat. Her emotions and meanings,
running in your nerves! Merely
memories you suppressed, you tell yourself!
Back in the day, we'd cut a lock of a

loved one's hair to twist into a wreath, a
token of the fine, dendritic
seine we cast upon experience.
You were thinking of unspoken thoughts.
Think how much of her you captured unknowing.
Think how narrowly the beam of
conscious awareness plays across the field
perception opens to it, across
remembrance's deep and recursively folded layers.
Just outside that tiny circle,

she has been waiting. She couldn't tell you. In that
pile of leaves and stems and seeds you
rolled into little sticks and burned was her voice.
You will never hear it again.
But, listen: I am a mother, and she, if she'd lived,
might have given birth to your children;
we begin in pain and separation.
Without them, there is no love.
Either we break up, or one of us dies.

What did you gain by denying that?"

My throat opens to the song of grief, a
hacking and hoarse rhythm that swells with
my surrender to it, consumes me, and fades.
I seem to stand at once outside and
in myself, watching the storm recede.
On my cheek, her cooling breath. My
eyes are fixed in hers. Her lips and mine move
silently together, like a
prayer. On this great field, filled with living, our
tongues' soft rasps meet and marry.

Canto XXXII: Her Long and Slender Touch

Just as Dante once upon a time was
chided for staring too fixedly at a
woman's smile – the smile of the woman who'd called him
out of the depths and up to his god, the
smile of a woman he'd long abandoned to death – his
guardian spirits fearful he'd
indulge in idolatry of incarnation:
so, reminders reach me from
beyond the play of shared body fluids,
electric rhythms, chemical messaging,

insisting this inner world I think I've recovered,
the ramifications of a skinny
California girl – of whom I've wished they
all could be – is but the other
extreme of the pendulum's swing from idiot me,
omnivorously absorbed in trees and
bugs and dirt and birds and scents on the wind, not
many hours ago on waking
to this paradise where all is present and
it's so easy to lose oneself.

Waking by stages: first, from the feverish nightmare of
hell's closed circles into

purgatory's weaving befuddlements; next, like
one reluctant to leave warm sheets who
semi-consciously prolongs his doze, he
passively witnesses all and sundry the
senses bring flooding in; with consciousness riding
ineluctably on the flood, he
staves it off a little longer by diving
headlong into reminiscence; and

here I am. "Where's Victoria?"
That's me, asking. "I'm right here, but
I am not the V you have in mind," says
she who brought me through the woods and
guided my somnambulistic ramble
back to them, or so it seems. "She's
sitting over there, beneath that oak."
It could have been a zag of light
falling on rough bark, a roughly z-shaped
afterimage lingering, or a

California girl's pale streak.
"Show me wonders," I call, and she
raises her arms and dances, slipping grace
around the oak's terrific mass, then
sinking on folding legs to sit full lotus
under it, facing me, her heels each
pulled in close beside her golden, downward-
pointing, upward-spreading pubis. Her

hands rest on her knees, palms up. Her gaze slants
left, just past her ghost of a smile.

An oak leaf falls from an upper branch to her shoulder,
its swooping progress illustrating
air resistance's effects upon a delicate,
semi-rigid membrane with complex
curvature and lobes so deep they almost
enclose oval spaces, twirling
to a halt against her bare, smooth skin, then
sliding and tumbling to her hand.
Her facial expression intensifies half a notch,
partly because it tickles and partly

because she knows what's going to happen next.
A huge limb comes crashing down.
I feel a jolt all through my body. A hand
at my elbow holds me back. "Steady."
Her head is on the other side, where I
can't see it. Her right leg's flung out straight.
Her left leg's still bent double; the knee's blunt arrow
points at me; the heel is jammed,
like some strange parody of a modest gesture,
against her crotch; her breasts are flattened

under a twist of the log that has mashed her torso.
By slow degrees, her skin turns dry
and white, so white it almost seems to glow,

as blood drains from it to pool in her back.
The sometimes quarreling, always imperious voices
that emanated from the center
of control are silent, and the great,
driving pumps of heart and lungs are
crushed and still. Without them, no supplies
arrive to replenish exhausted cells.

Uncollected, toxic wastes pile up.
Nothing comes to take them away.
Muscle fibers hook and pull together,
contracting tightly, then find they lack
the chemical energy to unhook, even
were a signal to do so to reach them.
Who would think that first among what's lost in
death is the power of relaxation? A
feral dog, worrying at the calf of
her bent leg, fails to unbend it. But

failing maintenance and replenishment, what was
fast wears out; later, when some
rats come by, her limbs respond to them.
They are not the only visitors.
Called from so far as ten miles away by
sulfides and acids she casts on the air,
blowflies, with their great, salmon eyes and
metallic body armor, lay their
clumps of eggs on wounds and other openings.

Finding refreshment in fluids exuded from

broken-down cells, they busily scrimmage for space. A
red-faced buzzard with a lovely,
white, hooked beak breaks open her right thigh.
Meanwhile, much as a city abandoned
by its civil and military authorities
quietens briefly – empty streets and
cautious, traumatized population homebound – but
soon small riots blossom and looting as
those upon whom the engines of social control have
hitherto ground their heaviest, spring free;

so, the milliards colonizing her gut, her
lungs and other interstices, whose
labor's contributions had been accepted (if
not their DNA) by the
imperial organism whose nature it was for
them to serve, no longer brought
by it the raw materials of their lives
or held back by its thriving order,
turn to take for themselves the meat that surrounds them.
So begins their time of plenty:

eating, excreting, and multiplying with
irrational exuberance;
adventuring to all corners of the realm
up arteries, veins, and lymphatic ducts

(now empty of all other moving traffic)
from which, before, they were forbidden;
mottling her pallid hide with lines and patches in
orange, red, blue, green, and
curved across her belly a streak of black; her
swelling belly. Putrescine,

cadaverine, methane, hydrogen sulfide,
ammonia, and other mercaptans off-gassed by
microbes consuming carbohydrates and proteins
balloon her skin, gurgle, and blatt from
existing orifices. The trunk and limbs lose
definition of muscles and joints, grow
smoothly tubular, crude as a sock puppet.
Somewhere about what might have been the
back of the left knee, a fissure opens
in the drying, over-stretched skin and

soon it is populated by the blowflies'
teeming, tawny, voracious larvae
and the wasps and beetles that prey on them. But
now the ground around the body is
dark and soaked with its escaping juices, a
flood so rich it causes a patch of
indian pipe, already drooping, to swoon. The
dessicating tissues toughen.
Maggots drop away and creep beneath the
leaf mold, into the soil that will shelter their

own next great transformation.
Nervously glaring around between each
plunge of its sharp beak, one last raven
picks at stragglers, then hops away.
Now the death becomes so much less lively.
The residue of internal organs
uneaten by microbes, insects, birds, or beasts
turns to slush and drains away. The
leathery tatters of skin and tissue that drape the
bones are slowly picked away by

weather's prying fingers of heat and cold,
wet and dry, with now and then some
help from an occasional gnawing tooth. The
rhythm lengthens. Light and dark pass
many times across a loosening flake
before it falls or is blown away.
At last, all that's left is the denuded, intricate
web of hydroxyapatite strands and
collagen fibrils – the structure of bones. The rhythm
lengthens. Putrefaction's acid

bath already has weakened the crystals' weave.
Now, bacteria eat the proteins,
leaving gaps and channels water enters,
freezing in cracks, expanding, thawing,
trickling, leaching calcium away.

Fungi and algae take their mite.
Some time, it's impossible to say when, this
many-handed diminution
reaches the point of invisibility, and
all that I am left to look at

is a carpet of leaves, of every shade from
palest yellow to deepest chocolate,
slowly becoming soil; indian pipes
nodding; a clump of trilliums that
wasn't there before; a trail of golden
chanterelles; the oak's hard bole, where
calcium rises. Watching all this, I've felt
everything you might imagine.
In my hand, from finger tip through palm, I
feel her long and slender touch.

Canto XXXIII: On the Beach

Hand in hand, we head off the path and
over that spot now empty of her and
yet so full I barely can push myself through it,
feet dragging through the leaves.
Time returns to a human scale. I want to
tell you that it does so "slowly," but
I can tell you little of what passed
before language returned to me.
The sun's slant casts the shadows of
the crowns of the trees we walk beneath,

far behind us; we walk in the shadows of trees we
have not passed beneath yet. Once more,
I walk into a darkening wood – this time,
in the care of selfless guides.
Unlike that other wood, the silence here is
broken only by forest noises: but
in my ears, lament inflects their cadences.
Everything sings its passing for me.
Having passed that place she rested last, I
walk at random, like one safe from

losing his way because wherever he is, is
where it is right for him to be.

My companions let me wander, helpful as
parents watching from a distance
necessary stumblings. Dante – how long
have I waited to hear your voice? –
offers encouragement: "Recall your sages' advice.
When the sacred grove is lost;
when the prayers and songs have been forgotten;
when the sacred dates are erased and

nobody quite knows how to build the altar;
then you will tell the story of these.
In the telling of it, you will find them.
Tell the story even though it *never solve the puzzle of her;*
is no more than words, your heart's not in it.
Some day, it will bring home meaning."
I don't know what he is talking about, and the
others gently try to shush him,
but I warm to hear him, because he cares and
cannot help it, caring's his nature.

Her voice follows his, from beside my heart, and
she, too, awkwardly muses, as
one whose throat is filled with another's grief.
"My career began with religion.
Religion led to money. Money led
to politics. Politics led to ruin.
Ruin led to a loving partnership.
I entered it through the gateless gate
of letting go of all that I had lost,

but not for once and always – no! –

every day, forever, letting go and
at the same time cherishing:
the price I pay myself for blessings received.
I foresee a day will come when
our sad species, misnamed *homo sapiens*
(in the wishful pride of our hearts!)
will be superseded, by creatures with powers
vaster than ours of observation,
recall, and empathetic understanding,
just as our linguistically agile,

fluid cognition leapfrogged our forebears over
poor old *homo heidelbergensis*,
because we could preserve within ourselves
a greater part of our dearly departed.
What you've witnessed was, and is not, and is."
Statius says, "I wish I'd said that."
"You still here? I wish you'd said it, too,"
she says, as I step out from beneath the
trees and onto a narrow, sandy path through
waist high grasses. Underfoot, the

sand yields to my steps more firmly than the
spongy pine needle duff that
I just left; that's how I know it's sand
hidden in the grasses' shadow

deep in the bottom of earth's shadow's cone this
clear, clear, moonless night.
In the forest, darkness submerged and confined us.
Here, it's receded waist deep
among the grasses part of me wades through and
part glides above as if floating.

Much farther ahead and to each side than
sight can penetrate, grass stalks
nod and ripple, barely, now and then,
here and there, under speckled blackness, a
stark and expansive vista, sketched with the thinnest
wash of photons. The grief that clung
around me through the woods like a hot cloak
not quite dissipates, rather, it opens,
letting in the barely stirring airs that
taking moisture leave coolness.

Several hundred yards of silent walking, and
I'm as alone as it's given to be. The
path's packed sand gives way to softer footing.
I meander through ever sparser
tufts of vegetation until I'm standing
before the waters. Distant, the city.
Quiet, quiet, quiet, quiet, quiet;
hush, hush, hush, hush
say the waters that fill this crescent I stand on.
My breaths join their flow and ebb.

How many angels can dance on the head of a pin?
How many atoms compose a star? The
night is replete with angels dancing on pinpricks.
In between them, not exactly
nothing, but nothing perceptible to me.
Thousands or millions of years ago, or
maybe only minutes or hours, one
particularly brilliant point
flung the particular brilliance that bounces off the
gently heaving surface tension

stretching out before me into my eyes, a
streak across the starlit bay,
thin and silvery, cold. It comes to me:
nothing cares to harm or love me; the
great crescent of tiny grains I stand on, the
great, distant, sparkling dance,
all are perfect in their indifference to me;
only the city's warmth at my back,
confused and steady, carries love to me and
all I carry into the void.

Fomite

A fomite is a medium capable of transmitting infectious organisms from one individual to another.

"The activity of art is based on the capacity of people to be infected by the feelings of others." Tolstoy, What Is Art?

Writing a review on Amazon, Good Reads, Shelfari, Library Thing or other social media sites for readers will help the progress of independent publishing. To submit a review, go to the book page on any of the sites and follow the links for reviews. Books from independent presses rely on reader to reader communications.

For more information or to order any of our books, visit http://www.fomitepress.com/FOMITE/Our_Books.html

Nothing Beside Remains
Jaysinh Birjépatil

The Way None of This Happened
Mike Breiner

Summer on the Cold War Planet
Paula Closson Buck

Foreign Tales of Exemplum and Woe
J. C. Ellefson

Free Fall/Caída libre
Tina Escaja

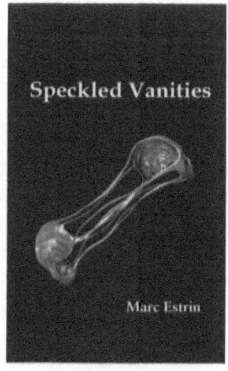

Speckled Vanities
Marc Estrin

Off to the Next Wherever
John Michael Flynn

Derail This Train Wreck
Daniel Forbes

Semitones
Derek Furr

Where There Are Two or More
Elizabeth Genovise

Snake in the Spine, Wolf in the Heart
Barry Goldensohn

The Three Lives of Jonathan Force
Richard Hawley

Father Figure
Lamar Herrin

In A Family Way
Zeke Jarvis

A Rising Tide of People Swept Away
Scott Archer Jones

Fomite

A Free, Unsullied Land
Maggie Kast

Shadowboxing With Bukowski
Darrell Kastin

Feminist on Fire
Coleen Kearon

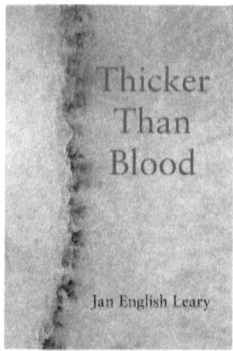

Thicker Than Blood
Jan English Leary

A Guide to the Western Slopes
Roger Lebovitz

Confessions of a Carnivore
Diane Lefer

Born Speaking Lies
Rob Lenihan

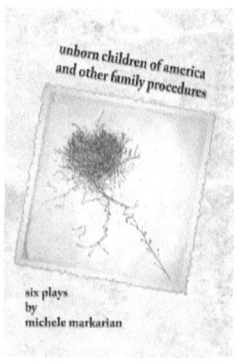

Unborn Children of America
Michele Markarian

Interrogations
Martin Ott

Fomite

Connecting the Dots to Shangrila
Joseph D. Reich

Shirtwaist
Delia Bell Robinson

Isles of the Blind
Robert Rosenberg

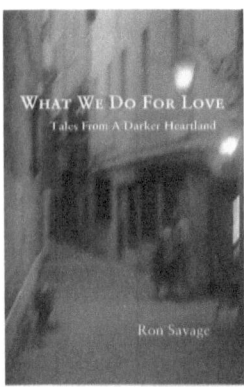
What We Do For Love
Ron Savage

Bread & Sentences
Peter Schumann

Faust 3
Peter Schumann

Principles of Navigation
Lynn Sloan

A Great Fullness
Bob Sommer

Industrial Oz
Scott T. Starbuck

Fomite

Among Angelic Orders
Susan Thomas

A Day in the Life
Tom Walker

The Inconveniece of the Wings
Silas Dent Zobal

More Titles from Fomite...

Joshua Amses — Raven or Crow

Joshua Amses — The Moment Before an Injury

Jaysinh Birjepatel — The Good Muslim of Jackson Heights

Antonello Borra — Alfabestiario

Antonello Borra — AlphaBetaBestiaro

Jay Boyer — Flight

David Brizer — Victor Rand

David Cavanagh — Cycling in Plato's Cave

Dan Chodorkoff — Loisada

Michael Cocchiarale — Still Time

James Connolly — Picking Up the Bodies

Greg Delanty — Loosestrife

Catherine Zobal Dent — Unfinished Stories of Girls

Mason Drukman — Drawing on Life

Fomite

Zdravka Evtimova —Carts and Other Stories
Zdravka Evtimova — Sinfonia Bulgarica
Anna Faktorovich — Improvisational Arguments
Derek Furr — Suite for Three Voices
Stephen Goldberg — Screwed and Other Plays
Barry Goldensohn — The Hundred Yard Dash Man
Barry Goldensohn — The Listener Aspires to the Condition of Music
R. L. Green When — You Remember Deir Yassin
Greg Guma — Dons of Time
Andrei Guriuanu — Body of Work
Ron Jacobs — All the Sinners Saints
Ron Jacobs — Short Order Frame Up
Ron Jacobs — The Co-conspirator's Tale
Kate MaGill — Roadworthy Creature, Roadworthy Craft
Tony Magistrale — Entanglements
Gary Miller — Museum of the Americas
Ilan Mochari — Zinsky the Obscure
Jennifer Anne Moses — Visiting Hours
Sherry Olson — Four-Way Stop
Andy Potok — My Father's Keeper
Janice Miller Potter — Meanwell
Jack Pulaski — Love's Labours
Charles Rafferty — Saturday Night at Magellan's
Joseph D. Reich — The Hole That Runs Through Utopia
Joseph D. Reich — The Housing Market
Joseph D. Reich — The Derivation of Cowboys and Indians
Kathryn Roberts — Companion Plants
David Schein — My Murder and Other Local News

Peter Schumann — Planet Kasper, Volumes One and Two

Fred Skolnik — Rafi's World

Lynn Sloan — Principles of Navigation

L.E. Smith — The Consequence of Gesture

L.E. Smith — Views Cost Extra

L.E. Smith — Travers' Inferno

Susan Thomas — The Empty Notebook Interrogates Itself

Tom Walker — Signed Confessions

Sharon Webster — Everyone Lives Here

Susan V. Weiss —My God, What Have We Done?

Tony Whedon — The Tres Riches Heures

Tony Whedon — The Falkland Quartet

Peter M. Wheelwright — As It Is On Earth

Suzie Wizowaty —The Return of Jason Green

www.ingramcontent.com/pod-product-compliance
Lightning Source LLC
Chambersburg PA
CBHW021433080526
44588CB00009B/512